Understanding the EU Budget

By Ben Patterson

Searching finance

First published 2011 by Searching Finance Ltd, 8 Whitehall Road, London W7 2JE, UK

ISBN: 978-1-907720-23-9

Typeset by: Deirdré Gyenes

Understanding the EU Budget

By Ben Patterson

Searching
finance

About Ben Patterson

Ben Patterson was a journalist, lecturer and a London borough councillor before Britain joined what was then the European Community, when he became Deputy Head of the European Parliament's London Office. In 1979 he was elected Member of the European Parliament for Kent West, sitting on a number of the Parliament's committees – including its Budgetary Control Committee – before becoming a Vice-chairman of the Economic and Monetary Committee in 1992. Earlier, as a member of that committee, he had been Parliament's *rapporteur* on the Single Market programme. Between 1992 and 1994 he was a Bureau Member of the Group of the European People's Party.

From 1994 to 2004 he was Principal Administrator in Economic, Monetary and Budgetary Affairs Division of the European Parliament's Research Department, and from 1996 to 1998 on its Monetary Union Task-Force.

Ben was educated at Westminster School, Trinity College Cambridge and the LSE, studying languages and economics. He has been a director of property-management and consultancy companies; and is married with two children.

Other publications by Ben Patterson

Direct Elections to the European Parliament (1974)
Powers of the European Parliament (1979)
Purse-Strings of Europe (1979)
Vredeling and All That (1984)
Europe and Employment (1984)
VAT: The Zero Rate Issue (1988)
European Monetary Union (1991)
A European Currency: on track for 1999? (1994)
Options for a Definitive VAT System (1995)
The Co-ordination of National Fiscal Policies (1996)
The Consequences of Abolishing Duty Free (1997)
Adjusting to Asymmetric Shocks (1998)
The Feasibility of a 'Tobin Tax' (1999)
The Determination of Interest Rates (1999)
Exchange Rates and Monetary Policy (2000)
Tax Co-ordination in the EU (2002)
Background to the Euro (2003)
Public Debt (2003)
The Euro: Success or Failure? (2006)

About Searching Finance

Searching Finance Ltd is a dynamic new voice in knowledge provision for the financial services and related professional sectors. Our mission is to provide expert, highly relevant and actionable information and analysis, written by professionals, for professionals. For more information, please visit www.searchingfinance.com

Acknowledgement

My great thanks to Richard Ashworth MEP, spokesman for the ECR Group in the European Parliament on the special parliamentary committee preparing the 2014–2020 financial framework, for his valuable comments on the draft of this study, and for keeping me informed of the latest developments.

CONTENTS

Understanding the EU Budget

List of tables and figures

Introduction

In January 1979 the London Information Office of the European Parliament published a short pamphlet entitled *Purse-strings of Europe: the European Parliament and the Community Budget*. I had written it to provide background briefing on one of the Parliament's two main powers at that time – to amend or reject the Budget – in preparation for the first European Elections later that year.

In 1978 the total Community Budget, covering the then nine Member States, came to 12.3bn European Units of Account (an artificial basket of currencies then used in budgetary calculations), which converted into £8.2bn. About three-quarters of the total was devoted to only one sector: agriculture; and this spending was then defined as 'compulsory' – i.e. those budgetary lines could not easily be amended, because they derived from the level of agricultural prices decided earlier at the Spring Price Review. The remaining quarter of the Budget, the 'non-compulsory' section, could be amended by the Parliament, subject to a 'maximum rate' of increase.

By 2010 what had become the Budget of the European Union of 27 Member States came to a total of over €141.5bn, or about £122.7bn. Of this, the agricultural sector now took only about 40%, much of it for 'environmental management' rather than price support. The big new area of spending was 'cohesion' and the 'structural funds' – largely aid to poorer countries and regions – which accounted for about 45% of the total. The European Parliament, in addition to its power of total rejection, now had powers of amendment over virtually the whole.

There had also been big changes on the revenue side. Whereas in 1978 about 56% had come from customs duties and levies on products coming into the Community from outside, and virtually all the rest from the 'Value Added Tax element', in 2010 over three-quarters of the revenue came from direct payments by Member States, based on their Gross National Income (GNI). Customs duties and a levy on sugar provided only 12% of the total, and VAT even less.

One key feature had not changed, though: the Budget has to balance. There is no question of running a budget deficit or incurring a public sector borrowing requirement. Unlike its Member States, the EU can have no resulting public debt. In consequence, Budgets are presented primarily in terms of expenditure – the taxation to cover it is assumed to be automatic.

Judging by the poor British turnout in the 1979 European Elections, my efforts to popularise the budgetary powers of the European Parliament were not particularly successful. Not long afterwards, however, the subject of the Budget exploded onto the political scene as the 'war of Maggie's money', a war which did not end until the final settlement of the UK's budget rebate at Fontainebleau in 1984; and the issue has been simmering below the surface of British politics ever since. The controversy in late 2010 over the proposed 2011 Budget – should it go up by 6.7%, 2.91% or nothing at all? – had a high media profile. Given a 2.91% increase, Britain's share, it was alleged, could alternatively finance 6,022 NHS doctors, 12,666 NHS nurses 14,636 police constables or 22,333 Army privates, at a time when the need for austerity meant reductions in all these domestic categories.

Such alarms and excursions over a sum which, in total, comes to only around 1% of the EU's GDP are, at first sight, somewhat difficult to justify – certainly when compared to UK public spending touching 50% of GDP. Several factors nevertheless make the EU Budget an easy target.

First, there is a widespread impression that it gives rise to – in the words of the Institute of Directors' Director General, Sir

John Hoskyns, in 1989 – "pilfering on an heroic scale". The fact that the EU's Court of Auditors has, year after year, failed to give the accounts a clean bill of health has not helped, despite the fact that the fault has largely lain at the door of the national governments which administer the bulk of EU funds, and which have often failed to provide proper statistics. And it is certainly true that, following the refusal of the European Parliament in the late 1990s to sign off the accounts and the publication of two investigative reports commissioned by the Parliament, the entire Commission was forced to resign. The first report "could not find a single person showing the slightest sense of responsibility".

Perhaps the most important reason for the Budget's vulnerability, however, is the opaqueness of its structure and of the EU's budgetary procedures. Each year the budgetary authority – that is, the EU Council of Ministers and the European Parliament acting together to a timetable established by the Treaty – vote on proposals from the Commission, classified as 'commitment appropriations' and 'payment appropriations'. The latter pay for multiannual programmes entered under the former. The whole annual procedure also takes place in the context of a five- to seven-year 'financial framework' and of a detailed 'financial regulation', and regulations adopted and frequently changed under the Union's legislative procedures.

Then there are the follow-up procedures: the reports of the Court of Auditors and the European Parliament's report and vote on the 'discharge', which attempt to establish how far actual expenditures have been made legally and have matched those voted in the original Budget. This is not a straightforward exercise. National projects for which money has been allocated can fail to materialise or be subject to long delays. Spending money from the Budget generally requires an appropriate legal instrument, which for some reason may not have been adopted. There can be transfers from one budgetary line to another. There are

3

usually supplementary budgets. The margins of error have in the past been such as to make a precise figure like 2.91% seem fanciful. Indeed some years on the European Parliament's Budgetary Control Committee tempted me to conclude that EU Budgets as published are largely works of fiction. In addition, past Budgets have involved such surreal concepts as 'negative expenditure',[1] and special 'green' exchange rates for trade in agricultural products.

And finally, in the Commission's own words,[2] the "opaque and complex" way the Budget is financed "creates a tension which poisons every budgetary debate".

It would be a mistake, nevertheless, to decide that the EU Budget is beyond clarification. Updating *Purse-strings of Europe* to take account of developments since 1979 is perhaps a worthwhile task, particularly since the subject is becoming topical as negotiations take place to establish a new multiannual financial framework (MFF): how much the EU will be able to spend between 2014 and 2020, and how much British taxpayers will have to contribute.

However small the net sum as a proportion of total public expenditure, British taxpayers deserve as good an explanation as can be provided of how the money they pay to Europe is raised and spent on their behalf.

---

[1] This was how the so-called 'co-responsibility' levies on milk production after 1977 were classified.

[2] *Financing the EU Budget: report on the operation of the own resources system* (Commission Staff Working Paper SEC(2011) 876 final of 29.6.2 011).

Chapter 1
Three key questions

Searching finance

To start this examination of the EU Budget, three key questions need to be discussed:

1   Why have an EU Budget at all?
2   How large should it be? and
3   Where does the money come from?

Why have an EU Budget at all?

In the disputes about the UK's contribution to the European Community Budget in the early 1980s, Prime Minister Margaret Thatcher shocked her colleagues with the widely-reported demand: "I want my money back". This phrase encapsulated what was thought on the Continent to be two serious heresies. First, the money was not considered to be hers (or Britain's) at all, but the 'own resources' of the Community. And secondly, if every country were to demand its *juste retour*, with money being paid into the Budget only to be paid back in some way, what was the point of having the Budget in the first place?

Clearly, if there is to be an administration for the European Union – institutions with staff, offices and other linked expenses – there has to be a budget of some kind. Contrary to popular belief, however, the size of the so-called 'Brussels bureaucracy' is tiny when compared to other administrations: some 25,000 officials in total, compared, for example, to the roughly 45,000 employed by the single UK local authority of Kent County Council (KCC). The Commission's estimated administrative budget for 2011 comes to €8.5bn out of the €142bn total. That of all the other institutions comes to roughly another €3bn, by far the largest component of which, in the case of the European Parliament, is the cost of operating in 23 languages. KCC's budget is not far short of this at £2.4bn (€2.9bn).

The rest is the operational budget, most of which is spent on programmes and projects within the 27 Member States themselves. For this, a number of justifications can be advanced.

Justifications

By far the largest item of operational expenditure in the years following the entry into force of the Rome Treaty in 1958 was the Common Agricultural Policy (CAP) – one of the two main sectoral policies established by the Treaty, the other being transport.[3] As original Article 38 of the Treaty stated, the primary object of the CAP was that the common market should "extend to agriculture and trade in agricultural products"; and in order for this to take place, the various national systems for supporting agriculture had to be replaced by a single system. Some countries, like the UK, then supported farmers by direct 'deficiency payments' from the taxpayer. However, the system chosen for the CAP (in devising which, of course, the UK could play no part) was to support market prices through intervention buying, taxes on imports and subsidies for exports. This made possible, in principle, the free movement of agricultural products between Member States.

The objective of a barrier-free internal market was also one of the justifications for creating, in the early Budgets, the Regional and Social Funds. The abolition of tariffs and quotas between Member States, it was argued, would increase competitive pressures on vulnerable regions and vulnerable employees. Competition policy would limit the scope for national subsidies; so the burden of adjustment should in part be borne by the common, European Community Budget.

At the same time, however, there were arguments for these Funds going beyond support for the internal market. In the case of the Regional Fund, for example, there was a strong element of redistribution. In a 'Europe of the Regions' the richer areas would help the poorer, not on the basis of redistribution within individual nations, but within the European Community as a

---

3   The coal and steel industries were, of course, already organised under the provisions of the 1951 Treaty of Paris, which established the European Coal and Steel Community (ECSC).

whole.[4] Similarly, the Social Fund aimed to "improve employ-ment opportunities for workers in the internal market and to contribute thereby to raising the standard of living...".[5] These were stand-alone economic and social objectives.

In later Budgets, the element of redistribution became more explicit. The so-called 'cohesion funds' were created for the express purpose of transferring resources – in this case, to nations as a whole as part of the agreements made on their accession to the Community. The consequent inflow of funds into, for exam-ple, Spain, was intended to help their economies catch up with those of existing Member States.

Behind other elements of the Budget has lain the justification of 'added value': as a result of economies of scale and the avoid-ance of duplication, expenditure made jointly would be more cost-effective than expenditure made separately. This has applied to a large number of budgetary lines in such fields as research, the creation of pan-European transport, energy and information networks (the TENs) and the spreading of best practice in the fields of training and innovation. It has also been part of the justi-fication for expenditure on external policies, notably assistance to developing countries, humanitarian aid and, more recently, the common foreign and security policy. Interestingly, in the one area where the added value argument might have been considered particularly strong, defence procurement, the EU Budget has played no part.

The added value argument, and the economic case for captur-ing externalities, has also played a part in the rising proportion of expenditure on environmental protection. The obvious fact

---

4 The redistributive effect of the Community Budget when the Regional Fund was created was actually negative: poorer countries such as Italy were net contributors; richer countries such as the Netherlands and France net recipients.
5 Original Article 146 of the Treaty.

that 'pollution knows no frontiers' had, by the late 1980s, already given rise to an increasing volume of legislation in the field. By the turn of the millennium a growing proportion of expenditure on agriculture itself was taking the form of aid to 'manage the rural environment' rather than simple price support. The need to control population movements – notably immigration into the EU – provides a similar example: protecting the external borders of the Union against illegal immigration falls naturally on Member States with external borders, but the consequences of success or failure are shared.

Finally, there have been certain smaller lines of expenditure which have been considered self-justifying – the creation in 1978, for example, of the European Community (now Union) Youth Orchestra. The objective of schemes in the educational field such as ERASMUS[6] has been to create a sense of European identity or solidarity, notably among younger generations.

Objections

Taken on their own, these justifications for the EU's operational budget clearly carry weight. The principal objection to them, however, has been that expenditures have in practice not always been made in accordance with the stated objectives, but rather in accordance with the denigrated principle of *juste retour*. As the Commission has noted in its 2010 Budget Review:[7]

---

6   Started in 1987, ERASMUS has since enabled more than 2.2m students, as well as 250,000 higher education teachers and other staff since 1997, to participate in exchange schemes involving higher education institutions both within the EU and in other countries (a total of 33 countries now participate).

7   Communication from the Commission to the European Parliament, the Council, the European Economic and Social Committee, the Committee of the Regions and national parliaments (COM(2010) 700 final).

"The concentration on the issue of 'net balances' meant that programmes were skewed to maximise the ability to put a 'national flag' on spending in advance."

In the case of the structural funds (the old regional and social funds plus the former 'guidance' section of the CAP), for example, Member States have found themselves promoting projects eligible for EU finance, not on the basis of merit, but merely in order to receive money back from the EU Budget. The resulting distortions – the exact opposite of added value – would probably have been more widespread had not there been a requirement for national, regional or local authorities to put up 'matching money' where projects receive EU finance.

But the need for matching money has also had damaging consequences. As the Court of Auditors has continually pointed out in its annual reports, substantial sums for payment voted in the Budget have remained unspent at the end of each year, one reason being that national or local authorities have been unable to afford their contributions. An investigation carried out by the *Financial Times* found that "the EU has paid out only 10% of €347bn allocated by its flagship [structural] fund up to 2013, more than halfway through its seven-year spending cycle."[8]

There is perhaps a case, therefore, for 'repatriating' parts of the EU Budget; and, indeed, one of the prime targets for repatriation has been the 40% currently devoted to agriculture. This would reduce the overall size of the Budget and/or allow resources to be re-allocated to projects likely to improve the EU's international competitivity, notably the research budget. Nevertheless, allowing each Member State to support its own farmers – or, of course, not to support them at all – has dangers. If farmers in, say, the UK were then to receive substantially less government support than those in, say, France, competition between them would be

---

8 'EU growth funds lie idle under red tape', Financial Times 29 November 2010.

thought unfair, leading to pressure for the re-imposition of internal tariffs or quotas. The common market in agricultural products could be destroyed.

It is also worth noting that an end to the CAP would certainly also mean an end to the UK budget rebate – an issue to be discussed later.

How big? The Budget and fiscal policy

The European Union Budget, unlike that of its Member States, is one of which Adam Smith (though not John Maynard Keynes) would probably have approved. First, it is relatively frugal, amounting to around only 1% of GDP (that is, about €235 per head of the population), compared to between 40% and 50% in the case of the national budgets. And second, it is required to balance from year to year.

One consequence of this second feature is that there can never be an annual borrowing requirement, creating EU public debt. Also in consequence, however, there can be no EU-level fiscal policy, either automatic (the operation of fiscal stabilisers) or discretionary (tax cuts or public works to stimulate demand and employment in times of recession, or higher tax rates to damp down inflationary pressures in times of boom). In fact the fiscal effect of the EU budget, though small, is pro-cyclical.

The situation, then, is effectively the reverse of that in the United States, where the Federal budget can, and does, run substantial deficits, but where State budgets must in principle balance. Many would say that this is no bad thing.

The impossibility of operating fiscal policy at EU level, however, has created certain problems, particularly for the euro area. First, and most obviously, it has meant that mechanisms have had to be devised to co-ordinate the fiscal policies of the participating countries, both in an attempt to create an 'aggregate fiscal stance' and to prevent fiscally lax countries from running up large public debts. These were the purposes of the 'multilateral surveillance' and 'excessive deficit' procedures established by the Maastricht Treaty (which apply to all EU Member States, not just those in the euro area), and the so-called Stability and Growth Pact. As we have seen, these mechanisms have proved staggeringly ineffective.

Second, in the absence of either an EU- or euro area-level fiscal policy, and in the light of the failure to control national fiscal policies, added pressure has been placed on monetary policy, the responsibility within the euro area of the independent European Central Bank (ECB). The shortcomings of a 'one size fits all' structure of interest rates has been emphasised, and the ECB itself has had to enter the markets for national public debt, arguably in breach of the 'no bail-out' provision of the Treaty. As was observed in a pre-EMU report by an independent group of economists, published by the Commission in 1993, *Stable Money – Sound Finances*,[9]

> "Without major changes, European economic and monetary union would…have a particular feature which is unique in history: a single monetary policy coupled with largely decentralised fiscal policies. One of the core issues for the future is whether European union will also need a big central budget…"

Proposals for an increase in the size of the EU Budget sufficient to make feasible an EU- or euro area-level fiscal policy were

---

9   *Stable Money – Sound Finances: Community public finance in the perspective of EMU (European Economy*, no. 53, European Commission, 1993). The experts included Professor Charles Goodhart from the London School of Economics and the Institute of Fiscal Studies (IFS), and Stephen Smith, also from the IFS.

already on the table in 1977. The MacDougall report,[10] produced at the request of the Commission, recommended increasing the Budget from the then 1.2% of Community GDP to 2–2.5% in a 'pre-federal' stage, rising to 5–7% and beyond as integration progressed. MacDougall's calculations were, of course, based on a Community of only nine Member States, between which economic disparities were relatively small. Figures on the same basis covering the present 27 Member States of the EU would almost certainly be significantly greater.

Such proposals, of course, are a very long way indeed from being accepted, either within the EU as a whole or within the euro area. The decentralisation of fiscal policy is considered a key application of the 'subsidiarity' principle written into the Treaty: reserving the power of decision to the most local level commensurate with efficiency. If anything, the prevailing mood is to restrict the EU Budget to a level at or below 1% of GDP.

Balancing the budget

There is also the question, however, of whether the requirement that the Budget balance from year to year should be modified, leading to the possibility of issuing EU public debt. In this case, recent events have made such a development less problematic. The rescue funds hastily assembled to meet the Greek debt crisis, and then the €17.7bn European Financial Stability Fund (EFSF), have depended on contributions and guarantees from Member States. But there is also the €60bn European Financial Stability Mechanism (EFSM), created in 2010 under the auspices of the European Commission, which are guaranteed on the EU Budget – an "innovative use of the Budget to support an urgent policy

---

[10] *Report of the Study Group on the Role of Public Finance in European Integration* by Sir Donald MacDougall (chairman) Vol.1: General Report (Office for Official Publications of the European Communities, April 1977).

need"[11], in the Commission's own words. The initial €5bn issue of EFSM euro-bonds at the beginning of 2011, earmarked for the Irish rescue package, was four times over-subscribed. Despite the relatively low yield of 2.5% on bonds maturing at the end of 2015 – the yield on five-year Irish bonds at the time was just below 8% – the markets clearly considered that the EU's credit rating made them excellent investments.

Whether euro-bond issues should be the result of meeting a budgetary borrowing requirement is, of course, a separate issue. Though the development of debt finance has historically proved a valuable tool – enabling Britain to fight and win the Napoleonic and other wars against France in the 18th and early 19th centuries, for example – another lesson of history is that unbalanced budgets are a slippery slope. As in the case of UK Chancellor of the Exchequer Gordon Brown's 'golden rule', whereby borrowing should only be used to finance investment, good intentions are easily forgotten when public finances get 'blown off course'. Borrowing, rather than taxation, is soon used to finance current spending; and towards the bottom of the slope, borrowing becomes the main way of financing the interest on the previous borrowing. No-one can be absolutely certain that the EU itself would not fall into such a trap. Better, perhaps, not to put temptation in its way.[12]

On the other hand, if something like a 'golden rule' could be effectively imposed, issuing such EU bonds could be a source of funds for capital projects, supplementing the facilities already

---

[11] In the 2010 'Budget Review'.

[12] Actually, as the Court of Auditors pointed out in its report for 1986, the Commission had already found a way of closing budget deficits by borrowing via 'refundable advances' in 1984 and 'non-refundable advances' in 1985, and by 'carrying over' expenditure for the disposal of butter surpluses to later years. These practices, the Court commented, meant that the Community was "mortgaging more and more of its future". (Court of Auditors' Report for 1986, General Matters, paras 1.7 and 1.8).

provided by the European Investment Bank (EIB). Proposals to this effect have from time to time been made by Commissioners and others, though Member State governments have so far firmly rejected such a large and (as Germany has argued) potentially inflationary expansion of the EU's role.

Where does the money come from?

From the beginnings of what is now the European Union the objective of those who drafted the Treaties was that the organisation's budget should be self-financing: that is, should not be dependent on transfers from the national budgets. This was indeed so in the case of the European Coal and Steel Community (ECSC).

In the case of the European Economic Community (EEC), decisions taken in the late 1960s and 1970s were intended to replace transfers from national budgets with revenues which would automatically accrue to the Community without passing through national budgetary processes. The most obvious sources of such revenue – besides the small amounts coming from fines on companies in breach of competition law, income tax on Community *fonctionnaires* and various other sources such as the sale of publications – were the tariffs charged on imports and variable levies on agricultural imports, together with a levy on sugar production. By the end of the 1970s these were financing over half the Budget. Most of the rest, it was hoped, could be financed by the 'Value Added Tax element' (see Chapter 2): revenues from VAT, it was believed, accurately reflected Member States' ability to pay.

Both these sources of revenue, however, were soon of declining value. In the case of tariffs and levies, the funds generated were bound to fall as bilateral and multilateral trade agreements led to reduced tariffs.[13] In the case of VAT it became clear that, despite attempts to harmonise the VAT base, the tax was in practice not after all a good indicator of national wealth. In 1991 the VAT base as a percentage of GNP varied between 40.6% in Italy and over 67% in Ireland and Portugal. In 2005 the decision was taken to simplify the system and levy the VAT element at a uniform rate of 0.30% on the harmonised base. Even so it was found necessary to reduce this rate for Austria (0.225%), Germany (0.15%), the Netherlands (0.10%) and Sweden (0.10%). Moreover, the VAT base taken into account was capped at 50% of each Member State's Gross National Income (GNI).

As a result, as shown in Figure 1.1, over three-quarters of the Budget is today financed by applying a uniform rate directly to each country's GNI (and even then, Sweden and the Netherlands benefit from a GNI rebate). Theoretically, like the residual VAT element, still the EU's 'own resources', these funds are in practice straight transfers from national exchequers – the situation which the Union's founding fathers sought to avoid.

There have been attempts from time to time to identify sources of tax revenue for the EU which would be genuinely free from the control of national treasuries: for example, a tax on oil imports, a general CO_2 tax, a carbon-trading tax or a tax on inter-EU air travel. Taxes of this kind have the added appeal that they are linked to improving the environment of the EU as a whole. Also with its attractions is the most recent Commission proposal: a one-off tax of 0.2% on euro area bank assets, which would raise some €50bn to help fund the new European Stability Mechanism.

---

[13] A further complicating factor is the so-called 'Rotterdam effect': goods landed there are assumed, statistically, to have been imported into the Netherlands, although a large proportion are on their way to other countries. This affects the calculation of Member States' 'net budgetary balances'.

Figure 1.1: Sources of funding for the EU Budget 2000–2010

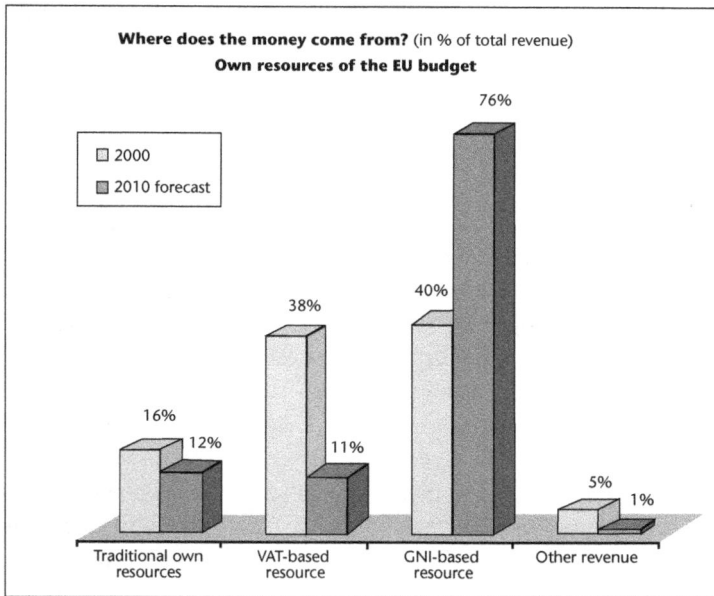

Source: EU Commission

More adventurous, but a great deal more controversial, have been proposals to 'federalise' some existing taxes: for example, allowing multinational firms to pay an EU corporate tax instead of the different national taxes.[14] Or the VAT element in current 'own

---

[14] It has been argued (for example in the 1992 Ruding Report, and earlier in the 1962 Neumark Report and the 1970 van den Tempel Report) that such an EU corporation tax would also have certain added advantages, unconnected with funding the Budget. Firms operating in several different Member States would need to deal with only one tax authority and pay only a single rate; and there would be no 'race to the bottom' in national corporate tax rates as Member States tried to attract inward investment. The Commission has, over the years, also made several proposals to allow EU companies to use a single consolidated base for computing tax on their EU-wide profits.

Understanding the EU Budget

resources' might be made a real VAT on transactions, rather than a notional rate on the harmonised base. VAT receipts would then look something like US Sales Tax receipts, with Federal and State charges shown separately. A rate of around 2% would fund EU expenditure at its current level.

The possibility of new 'own resources' was specifically provided for in the Lisbon Treaty. The relevant Article reads:

> "The Council, acting in accordance with a special legislative procedure, shall unanimously and after consulting the European Parliament adopt a decision laying down the provisions relating to the system of own resources of the Union. In this context it may establish new categories of own resources or abolish an existing category. That decision shall not enter into force until it is approved by the Member States in accordance with their respective constitutional requirements. The Council, acting by means of regulations in accordance with a special legislative procedure, shall lay down implementing measures for the Union's own resources system insofar as this is provided for in the decision adopted on the basis of the third paragraph. The Council shall act after obtaining the consent of the European Parliament."

Inevitably, of course, the scope and levels of such taxes would have to be decided, not by the UK House of Commons or the other national parliaments, but by the EU Council and the European Parliament.

Chapter 2
Historical background

Searching
finance

The Three Communities

The first embodiment of what is now the European Union was the European Coal and Steel Community (ECSC), which came into being when the Treaty of Paris entered into force in 1952. It was entirely self-financing. As Article 49 of the Treaty put it:

> "The High Authority is empowered to procure the funds it requires to carry out its tasks:
> - by imposing levies on the production of coal and steel;
> - by contracting loans.
> It may receive gifts."

The ECSC budget was largely devoted to measures for modernising the coal and steel industries in the six signatory countries.[15] Non-repayable grants were funded from levies. Funds raised by borrowing could only be used to make loans. (The Treaty did not make specific provision for the spending of gifts.)

The financial year covered by the ECSC Budget was established as the calendar year, a precedent carried on in the subsequent Budgets of the EEC and EURATOM, and eventually the European Union. The timetable established also provided a precedent. Each of the ECSC's institutions – High Authority,[16] Court, Council and Assembly[17] – was required to provide estimates for the following year by 1 July, which were consolidated by the Authority into a 'preliminary draft administrative budget'. At the same time a 'preliminary draft budget' covered "expenditure necessarily resulting from the Treaty" (what would later be called 'compulsory expenditure'). By 1 September these had to be before the Council

---

15 Belgium, France, Italy, Luxembourg, the Netherlands and West Germany.
16 The body later merged with the EEC and EURATOM Commissions to become what is now the European Union Commission.
17 This would eventually become the European Parliament. At this time it consisted of nominated members of the national parliaments. The Assembly (or Parliament) of the European Community, now the European Union, would not be directly elected until 1979.

which then established a 'draft budget' and a 'draft administrative budget', forwarding them to the Assembly by 5 October.

The Assembly then had the right, within 40 days, to propose amendments "by a majority of members" to the draft administrative budget, and 'modifications' to the draft budget by an "absolute majority of the votes cast". The Council could, within 15 days, accept these; or reject them by qualified majority, in which case the Budget went back to the Assembly for a second reading. This, too, had to take place within 15 days. Only changes (also confusingly called modifications) made by the Council to administrative expenditure amendments could be voted on again; and, to get its way, the Assembly needed a "majority of its members and three-fifths of the votes cast". A maximum rate of increase from year to year applied "in relation to expenditure of the same type".

The total expenditure of the ECSC in the early years was, of course, a small fraction of what would be in the later Budgets of the European Community and the EU: a mere US$50m in 1953.[18] In 1967 the administrative part of the ECSC Budget was merged with those of the other Communities – the EEC and the European Atomic Energy Community (EURATOM) – with the ECSC making a small contribution out of its own revenues (a lump sum of 5m EUA after 1977). The operational part, however, remained separate until the ECSC ceased to exist when the Paris Treaty lapsed in 2002. In the late 1980s it was running at some 300m ECU.

---

[18] Before 1978, the Budgets of the ECSC and later the EEC and EURATOM were expressed in European Units of Account (EUAs) equal to 'pre-Smithsonian Dollars', or 0.88867088 grams of fine gold. The exchange rates of this Unit against the national currencies involved were fixed, most at parities which soon grew wildly out of date. From 1978 the EUA was therefore redefined as a 'basket' of Member States' currencies, worth, at the time, about 42p. Shortly afterwards, following the creation of the European Monetary System in 1979, the EUA was replaced by the European Currency Unit (ECU), which, in turn, was replaced by the Euro at the beginning of 1999.

When the EEC and EURATOM came into being as a result of the 1957 Rome Treaties, the initial budgetary arrangements differed in one important respect from those of the ECSC: expenditure was financed by direct transfers from the six Member States' national budgets. In the case of the EEC, however, provision was also made for the Community, like the ECSC, eventually to have its 'own resources'.

The Treaty establishing the EEC provided for a budgetary procedure in most respects similar to that already operating in the case of the ECSC. Instead of presenting estimates in the form of an 'administrative budget' and a 'budget', the two were consolidated into a single proposal, divided, however, into "expenditure necessarily resulting from this Treaty or from acts adopted in accordance therewith" ('compulsory') and the rest ('non-compulsory'). What was still called 'the Assembly' had the right to propose 'amendments' to the non-compulsory lines, and 'modifications' to the compulsory ones, leading to procedures of voting in Assembly and Council on the model of those already applied in the ECSC.

In this original version of the Treaty the Assembly did not have the explicit right to reject the Budget as a whole. To obtain this power, it had to wait until a Treaty amendment in 1975, which provided that

> "acting by a majority of its Members and two-thirds of the votes cast, [it] may, if there are important reasons, reject the draft budget and ask for a new draft to be submitted to it".

The innocuous-sounding 'important reasons' phrase was actually critical. It was designed to prevent a Budget from being rejected by a coalition of opposing interests: some MEPs, for example, in favour of higher agricultural spending, some for lower. When what was by then the directly-elected European Parliament rejected the 1980 Budget, getting all sides behind a single reason needed considerable skill on the part of the *rapporteur*[19] and future Parliament President, the Dutch Socialist Piet Dankert.

Meanwhile, the Rome Treaty setting up EURATOM provided for separate 'operating' and 'research and investment' budgets which were directly funded by contributions from Member States according to national quotas which differed slightly, however, between the two budgets. The research and investment budget was required to show:

(a) commitment appropriations, covering a series of items which constitute a separate unit and form a coherent whole;

(b) payment appropriations which represent the maximum amount payable each year in respect of the commitments entered into under subparagraph (a).

This gave as good an explanation as any of the system which would in due course apply to the EU Budget as a whole.

The procedure for adopting the EURATOM budget then followed the model provided by the ECSC Treaty.

The Merger Treaty and 'own resources'

Although the ECSC, the EEC and EURATOM continued to exist as separate Communities (at least until the ECSC ceased to exist), important changes took place under the so-called Merger Treaty of 1965. Under this, the separate institutions of the three – High Authority/Commissions, Councils, Courts and Assemblies – were merged: in effect, a takeover by the institutions of the EEC.

---

[19] Once one of Parliament's specialist committees is made responsible for a particular matter – a Commission draft law, an 'own initiative' by the committee itself or, as in this case, the Community Budget – one of its members is appointed to pilot the business through its various parliamentary stages: the *rapporteur*.

Understanding the EU Budget

What had been called the 'European Communities' (and was still so-called in legal documents like the UK European Communities Act 1972) gradually became the 'European Community' until becoming the 'European Union' under the Maastricht Treaty of 1992.

On the financial side, there was also a merger of budgets. The administrative budget of the ECSC, the whole budget of the EEC and both the operating and research and investment budgets of EURATOM became the Budget of the European Communities.

Before the Merger Treaty could come into effect, however, there was the crisis of French President de Gaulle's 'empty chair' policy, and the subsequent Luxembourg Accords of January 1966. This was at its root a dispute about national sovereignty of the kind which has become familiar in British politics at least since the time of the Maastricht Treaty. Its immediate cause, however, was a dispute about financing, and especially the financing of agriculture. Accordingly, the Luxembourg agreement provided for "the financial regulation for agriculture" to be decided "by common consent", as well as the "common prices for milk, beef and veal, rice, sugar, olive oil and oil seeds". This meant that the three-quarters of the Budget devoted to the Common Agricultural Policy (the CAP) would already effectively be decided before the budgetary procedure itself could get under way.

The next major change to the budgetary system took place under Treaty amendments agreed on 22 April 1970. This incorporated a Council Decision of the previous day "on the Replacement of Financial Contributions from Member States by the Communities' own Resources". Beginning in 1971, all the proceeds of the variable levies on agricultural products would be paid directly into the revenue side of the Budget; and an increasing proportion of the proceeds from the Common External Tariff on goods from outside the Communities would be progressively transferred during a transition period ending in 1974. A 10% rebate to Member States would be made to cover the costs of collection.

As from 1975, 'own resources' were also to include a third element:

> "those accruing from the value added tax and obtained by applying a rate not exceeding 1 per cent to an assessment basis which is determined in a uniform manner for Member States according to Community rules".

There was, and still is, a lot of confusion as to what this actually meant. The sum resulting from applying 1% to the VAT base (the 'assessment basis') is not the same as 1% of the VAT actually paid in any particular country – the UK VAT base, for example, *includes* zero-rated transactions (though not those that are exempt), even though they raise no revenue. The methodology for calculating the sum is, in fact, complex. The starting point is the VAT actually collected in the Member States, and this is used to calculate a 'VAT gap': the shortfall from the theoretical VAT liability based on the VAT base. The gap is then paid out of other national revenue. A study to quantify and analyse the VAT gap in the EU-25 Member States, except Cyprus, published by the Commission in September 2009, estimated the gap between accrued VAT receipts and a theoretical net VAT liability to be an average of 13% for the period 2004–06.

In fact, the Achilles heel of this idea turned out to be the need to harmonise the VAT base. This meant that the same transactions had to be subject to VAT in all Member States, even if the rate was zero – the objective of the complex Sixth VAT Directive. This was not adopted until 1977, with the result that the VAT element of the Budget could not be applied until 1980. The Sixth Directive also contained a large number of exceptions and loopholes, leading to a long series of amending Directives in the years that followed.

It also soon became clear that there were significant variations between the size of Member States' 'black economies', within which not only the payment of VAT, but also appearance in the VAT base,

Understanding the EU Budget

was evaded. This, indeed, was found to be one reason for the defects of VAT as an indicator of national wealth, noted in Chapter 1.

The Court of Auditors and the Parliament

Perhaps the most important change to the budgetary system introduced by the 1975 reforms, however, was the creation of the Court of Auditors, which replaced the separate Audit Board of the EEC and the office of the ECSC auditor. As the Court's first report observed in 1978:

> "The principal distinctions between the Court and its predecessors are that the Court enjoys quasi-institutional status, its members are full-time, it has enhanced powers especially as regards the auditing of all Community income and expenditure and accounts (whether budgetised or not), it may start its work immediately expenditure has been committed, i.e. it need not wait until the accounts are closed, it is entitled to carry out on-the-spot audits in the Member States on its own initiative, it can make observations at any time on specific questions of its own choosing, it gives opinions at the request of any of the institutions, it gives opinions on financial legislation and it publishes its reports in the Official Journal."

Setting up the Court was also linked to another provision in the July 1975 Treaty: investing the European Parliament with the sole right of discharge.[20] Previously Council and Parliament had exercised this power jointly.

---

[20] Discharge is the decision by which the European Parliament, after having received recommendations from the Council, releases the Commission, as the body responsible for the implementation of the Budget, from any further liability in respect of its budget management, and brings the annual budgetary process to an end. Separate discharges are required for the administrative budgets of the other institutions.

The Court's annual reports, from its first on the 1977 Budget to its latest on that for 2010, together with its special reports (the results of audits dealing with specific subjects – there were 14 of these in 2010), have over the years subjected the Community and EU Budgets to a relentless scrutiny – ironically, one that has done much to bring the Commission, and with it the EU itself, into disrepute. The early reports provide evidence of an at times heated exchange of views between the Court and the Commission, with the Commission even challenging the authority of the Court: for example disputing the right of the Court to reply to the Commission's comments on the Court's findings.[21]

Despite a Commission statement in the second report – the first covering a full year – that it was "gratified at the climate of mutual confidence that has been established between itself and the Court of Auditors",[22] this tension continued unabated in the years that followed. In the 1980 report, for example, the Court records the Commission changing the arrangements for pre-publication consultations, but "without having informed the Court of an intention to do so".[23] For its part, the Commission had the year before regretted that "the Court did not pay more attention to the Commission's efforts to improve implementation of the Budget". The Court's "negative point of view" was doing "a disservice to Community integration".[24]

The changes made in 1975 also substantially increased the role of the European Parliament. Until then, the Community's 'budgetary authority' had been the Council. Now the authority was the Council and Parliament acting together. Parliament also acquired the two enhanced powers already mentioned – to reject the budget as a whole and to grant or refuse discharge. These were to

21 See the 1977 Report, Introduction, para.9.
22 See the 1978 Report, General Comments, Commission comments on paras 1.1 and 1.2. There is some suspicion that the remark was meant to be ironic.
23 See 1980 report, Introduction para.9.
24 See 1980 report, Introduction para.21.

Understanding the EU Budget

prove springboards for eventual amending powers over the whole of the budget under the Lisbon Treaty.

In 1978, Parliament's *rapporteur* on that year's Budget, the British MP Michael Shaw,[25] published a blow-by-blow account of the budgetary procedure as it emerged from the 1975 Treaty amendments;[26] and this gives a good account of the tensions between the two halves of the budgetary authority which would arise, in a much more acute form, in the years to come. Central to the disputes were Parliament's determination to reduce the proportion of the Budget devoted to the CAP in the face of what Shaw described as "the crude decision-making procedures within the Council which are not able to cope with the real needs of the Community".

The new powers were inherited by the first directly elected Parliament, which assembled in July 1979. Parliament, however, still only had real powers of detailed amendment over the so-called 'non-compulsory' sections of the Budget; and the classification of items as compulsory or non-compulsory was itself a matter of dispute: the Council, for example, had initially refused to admit that the Regional Fund was non-compulsory on the grounds that it had itself decided on a fixed three-year figure. By 1979 there was agreement on a non-compulsory classification. Even so, this only gave Parliament real amending powers over about a quarter of expenditure.

The rejection of the 1980 Budget by the Parliament at the end of 1979 was therefore more to show that, as an elected body, it now had to be taken seriously than any fundamental defect in the draft figures, which were similar to those of previous years.

---

25 At this time MEPs were still drawn from the membership of national parliaments: Michael Shaw was the MP for Scarborough. In 1994 he became Baron Shaw of Northstead.
26 *The European Parliament and the Community Budget* by Michael Shaw (European Conservative Group, June 1978).

As a member of Parliament's Budgets Committee at the time, the Labour MEP Richard Balfe recalled, "we were going to reject the Budget, whatever compromises the Council offered".[27] The result was that expenditure in 1980 was initially determined by the 'system of twelfths': a sum equal to a twelfth of the payment totals in the 1979 Budget could be spent in each month.[28] This system, the Court of Auditors observed in its 1980 report, "in certain respects lacked precision"; and, in practice, it did not unduly disrupt the pattern of Community spending. Parliament, however, had proved its point.

The UK rebate issue

Discussions concerning the European Community Budget in the early 1980s were dominated by the issue of the United Kingdom's net contribution – the 'war of Maggie's money'. The term 'net contribution' appeared nowhere in the legal framework of the Budget; it was one "fraught with significant conceptual and

---

[27] In *Memories of the first elected European Parliament* (Allendale, 2007). Balfe later became a Conservative.

[28] A more precise description of this 'system of twelfths' was contained in the Court of Auditors report on the 1980 budget:

"This procedure allows, for each chapter of the budget, commitments to be entered into during the first month up to one-quarter of total appropriations in the relevant chapter in the preceding financial year, with the limit increased by one-twelfth in each succeeding month, subject to an overall limit of the amount included in the draft budget for the new year. Payments may be made each month not exceeding one-twelfth of the appropriations in the relevant chapter of the preceding financial year or of the draft budget for the new year, whichever is less.

"At the request of the Commission, the Council may, after consulting the Parliament, authorise the simultaneous expenditure of two or more provisional twelfths."

(General Comments, paras 1.5 and 1.6)

accounting problems", in the later words of the Commission.[29] The Commission did, nevertheless, publish figures comparing the funds coming from particular Member States with the funds received by them under various Community programmes, producing rough 'net balances'. These showed the UK's net payments running at a higher proportion of Gross National Income (GNI) than that of the only other major – and richer – net contributor, West Germany.

The possibility of correcting for an adverse net balance was, in fact, already envisaged when the UK joined the Community in 1973.[30] Following the 1974–75 renegotiation by the Labour Government of Harold Wilson, a mechanism had actually been put in place, based not on net balance but on gross contributions. This did not make the issue go away. A final solution was only reached at Fontainebleau in 1984, and enacted in the own resources decision of May 1985.

The mechanism agreed at Fontainebleau applied exclusively to the UK. However, it was observed that the decision was based on the principle that

> "….any Member State sustaining a budgetary burden which is excessive in relation to its relative prosperity may benefit from a correction at the appropriate time".[31]

In 1984, three factors contributed to the UK's adverse position:

1. On the revenue side, the UK's higher propensity to import from outside the Community, resulting in high payments of levies and tariffs into the Budget. This was, however, of only marginal importance.

---

[29] See *Proposal for a Council Decision on the system of the European Communities' own resources* (COM(2004)501 of 3.8.2004).

[30] See *The United Kingdom and the European Communities* (Cmnd. 4715, HMSO July 1971).

[31] Presidency conclusions following the Fontainebleau European Council, 1984.

2. On the expenditure side, the UK's relatively low receipts under the Common Agricultural Policy, which was at that time 70% of the budget.
3. The UK's per capita income, which was in 1984 only 90.6% of the Community average.

The size of the Budget had risen by more than 400% during the eight years that followed British accession, so exacerbating the problem of Britain's share of the total. This rose from 8.8% in 1973 to over 20% by 1979, at a time when Britain accounted for only about 16% of Community GDP.

The Fontainebleau agreement was implemented in May 1985 by a Council Decision. The so-called UK correction mechanism provided for budget rebates equivalent to 66% of the UK's budgetary imbalance. The cost of financing the correction was shared between the other Member States according to their shares of VAT payments, except for West Germany, whose share was reduced by a third.

Budgetary discipline

In addition to settling the issue of the UK's net budgetary contributions, the Fontainebleau summit reached an agreement on the need for 'budgetary discipline'. This did not take the form of a legal text, but rather of a 'political agreement' asserting that "the rigorous rules which...govern budgetary policy in each member state shall also apply to the Budget of the Communities."[32] There should be a "reference framework for overall budgetary expenditure", a "financial guideline" for spending on agricultural support, and a commitment to observe the maximum rate of

---

[32] Conclusions of the Council on the measures necessary to guarantee the effective implementation of the conclusions of the European Council on Budgetary Discipline, 10446/84, Preamble.

increase in non-obligatory expenditure provided for in what was then Article 203 of the Treaty.[33]

The budgetary discipline agreement soon, however, brought the Council into direct conflict with the European Parliament. As one half of the budgetary authority, Parliament rejected the right of the other half, the Council, to take unilateral action – particularly since the 'discipline' appeared to apply only to that part of the Budget, the non-obligatory expenditure, over which the Parliament had powers of amendment, but not to the obligatory expenditure: i.e. that on agriculture. Taking the fight to the enemy, Parliament adopted a Budget for 1986 providing for increased non-obligatory expenditure far above the notional maximum rate, and also above the increased maximum the Council was prepared to concede. Apart from the issues of principle, Parliament argued that a substantial rise in spending was justified as the cost of the Community's enlargement to take in Greece, Portugal and Spain; and also that payment appropriations had to rise substantially to fund commitments already entered into: the 'cost of the past'.

The Council of Ministers' response was, by seven votes to three, to bring an action against the European Parliament before the Court of Justice. At the same time the UK, together with the Netherlands, Luxembourg, France and Germany, brought its own parallel action against the Parliament, an insurance against the "slight risk that the Court might find the Council's case to be inadmissible" (which, in the event, it did not).

---

33 Paragraph 9 of this Article read:
"A maximum rate of increase in relation to the expenditure of the same type to be incurred during the current year shall be fixed annually for the total expenditure other than that necessarily resulting from this Treaty or from acts adopted in accordance therewith."
This rate was to be worked out by the Commission, taking into account the trend rate of GDP growth in the Community, the "average variation in the budgets of the Member States" and changes in the cost of living. The article also made provision, however, for the maximum rate to be exceeded by agreement of the budgetary authorities.

Meanwhile, the Commission made it clear that it would implement the Budget as voted by the Parliament, pending the Court's judgment. Moreover, though still disputing the legality of the Budget, the UK did not withhold its payments as it might have done. A furious House of Commons Treasury and Civil Service Committee concluded that the budgetary discipline agreement "lacked authority" and, in the first year of its full application, had "not worked as intended".[34] The idea which the UK Government had advanced – that the interests of the net contributing countries would make budgetary discipline self-enforcing – had turned out to be "a chimaera".

The Court of Justice made its ruling on the case of the 1986 Budget in July that year.[35] It declared "void the act of the President of the European Parliament of 18 December 1985 whereby he declared that the Budget for 1986 had been finally adopted", on the grounds that the budgetary procedure for the year had yet to be completed: i.e. that Parliament and Council had not reached agreement on the maximum rate. The Court, however, pointedly remarked that it was "left with the impression that the respective positions taken by the two institutions could hardly have constituted a serious obstacle to the possibility of arriving at an agreement." Parliament had wanted 18.17% for commitment appropriations and 29.10% for payment appropriations, whereas the last proposals made by the Council were 17.02% and 24.46% respectively. The Court also ruled that all payments that had been made under the disputed Budget would stand.

Parliament's original objections were, in the event, partly vindicated when the Court of Auditor's report on the 1986 Budget appeared. The action against the Parliament had been taken

---

34 Fifth Report from the Treasury and Civil Service Committee of the House of Commons: *Budgetary Discipline in the European Community* (HMSO, 21 April 1986).

35 Judgment of 3.7.1986 — CASE 34/86.

because it was accused of voting for an excessive increase in non-agricultural spending. But the Court observed that

> "contrary to the political decisions taken at the European Summit in Fontainebleau in 1984, agricultural expenditure has grown – and may well continue to grow – at a rate which is much faster than that of own resources. This situation is mainly due to the almost unlimited amount of automatic support for prices that have been fixed at a very high level ...."[36]

Financial perspectives

The dispute on the 1986 Budget was not the only conflict between the two arms of the budgetary authority. They had become, year after year, at loggerheads over the size of the Budget and the priorities within it. At the end of 1984 the draft budget for 1985 was again rejected, and the system of twelfths applied until a Budget was finally approved in June. The 1986 budget, as described above, was the subject of litigation (Parliament and Commission later turned the tables by taking legal action against the Council for its failure to adopt the 1988 Budget in time). The 1987 Budget was not adopted until February of the same year resulting, once more, in application of the system of twelfths.

The Court of Auditors' report for that year also describes "disorder" in the "financial and regulatory situation", with 18% of the payments made in 1987 not charged to the 1987 Budget, and an actual deficit for the year of €6.25bn. The annual nature of the Budget was being "seriously undermined".

The Court cited, as an example, the management of the CAP:

> "By successively adjusting the timing of the agricultural financial year so as to fit the appropriations available, or by carrying over other items of expenditure to subsequent financial years, the Community has managed to maintain the semblance of

---

[36] Part I, Chapter 1, para 1.18.

a balanced budget. But such expedients have serious conse-quences for budgetary control."[37]

Apparently binding decisions on budgetary discipline, set by the national governments, lost "all meaning and effectiveness" when the continuity of accounting procedures from one financial year to another was not strictly observed.

As the Court concluded, a fundamental reform of the Community's budgetary procedure was required. Accordingly, in 1988, the Council and the Parliament concluded an 'inter-institutional agreement' (IIA), enabling the two wings of the budgetary authority to make decisions, in advance, for a period covering a number of years.[38] The first of these 'financial perspec-tives' – the so-called Delors I package, after the then President of the Commission – covered 1988–1992, and was designed to finance the budgetary consequences of the Single European Act and the '1992' programme for a Single Market. Thereafter Delors II covered 1993–1999, Agenda 2000 covered 2000–2006, and that currently in force 2007–2013.

The purposes of these multiannual financial frameworks were to set a maximum amount for future EU expenditure, both in total and by category; and also to lay down 'political priorities' as guidelines for its composition. For each programming period, the framework determined 'ceilings' (the maximum amounts both of commitment appropriations and payment appropria-tions) per 'heading' (the categories of expenditure) for each year. The annual budgetary procedure thereafter determined the exact level of expenditure and the breakdown between the various budget lines.

The present financial framework (2007–2013), for example, comprises six headings:

---

[37] Report of the Court of Auditors for 1987, General Matters, para. 1.9.

[38] The Commission had, in fact, already been publishing non-binding triennial financial estimates.

1. Sustainable growth:
   1a. Competitiveness for growth and employment;
   1b. Cohesion for growth and employment.
2. Preservation and management of natural resources.
3. Citizenship, freedom, security and justice:
   3a. Freedom, security and justice;
   3b. Citizenship.
4. The European Union as a global player.
5. Administration.
6. Compensations (related to the latest enlargement of the Union).

The annual level of payment appropriations has been capped by an 'own resources ceiling' of 1.24 % of the EU's GNI – although, in practice, annual expenditure has so far run well below this level.

Creation of a multiannual framework for Budgets did not, of course, end the tensions and fraught negotiations between the Community's institutions, and between Member States, on budgetary matters. During the negotiations leading to Delors II, for example, several governments objected to the projected substantial Budget increases on the grounds, once again, that the EU needed to observe the same degree of austerity in public spending that they themselves were having to impose – an argument that finds loud echoes as the negotiations for the 2014–2020 framework get under way. In the event, Delors II was agreed at the Edinburgh Summit in December 1992 – chaired by the UK Prime Minister, John Major – and envisaged substantial increases in the Budgets between then and 1999. Commitment appropriations were to rise from some ECU 69bn in 1993 to over ECU 84bn in 1999, and payment appropriations from just under ECU 66bn to over ECU 80bn. This represented a rise from 1.2% of GDP to 1.26%. The main areas of expansion were to be transfers under the Structural and Cohesion Funds to poorer Member States.

The budgetary decisions of 1988 also marked the end of VAT as the main budgetary revenue-raiser. The Fontainebleau Summit of 1984 had raised the maximum VAT call-in rate from the 1% agreed in 1975 to 1.4 %, with the possibility of a further rise to 1.6%. It was already becoming clear at the time, however, that VAT was a defective basis for funding the EU Budget, and that a new source of revenue would have to be found. In 1988 a major reform of the Community's finances broadened the composition of the Community's own resources by the creation of a new budget-balancing category of revenue based on the application of a percentage rate to Member States' gross national product (GNP).[39] This now provides the overwhelming bulk of the Budget's funding, with the VAT element having shrunk to relative unimportance (by 1999 the VAT call-in rate had, in any case, been reduced back to 1% and was successively cut to 0.5% from 2004).

Decisions were also taken in 1988 leading to long-term restrictions on the overall size of the Budget. A ceiling to the amount of own resources was agreed, which could rise to 1.2% of Community GNP by 1992. In 1992 the Edinburgh Council agreed to raise this to 1.21% by 1995 and to 1.27% by 1999.

Developments in the 1990s

The Community had also in 1988 undertaken a major reform of the CAP, which had substantial budgetary implications. As the Court of Auditor's Report for 1990 noted, it had become clear that the Community Budget was "entering an extremely difficult period, in which the agricultural guideline policy which was established in 1988 will be put under severe pressure". The report pointedly drew attention to the steps it had taken to evaluate the Commission's follow-up controls on agricultural spending in the years 1983–88.

---

39 As from 2002 GNP was replaced by gross national income (GNI).

The result was that

> "it was unclear what action, if any, had been taken to redress the weaknesses indicated.... Given the deficiencies of the system, the Commission has recently decided to abandon it entirely. Attempts during the past five years to develop a computerised system have so far come to nought [sic]."

The Court's 1990 report also noted that "major international developments such as the unification of the two Germanys and the opening up of Central and Eastern Europe are of potentially great significance for the Community budget".

The Court's report on 1991 began with a much fuller analysis of defects in "the management and auditing the Community's finances". In some cases, the fault lay in the "inadequate drafting of rules and regulations": for example, it was impossible to check whether price compensation aid to 'several million' beef, veal and olive oil producers had been properly spent. In other cases, organisational failure meant that errors were not detected and corrected. The 1992 report returned to the charge: examples of "insufficient checking by the Commission of legality and regulatory aspects of transactions" were to be found "throughout this report". In the case of the Structural Funds, for example, "much ineligible expenditure had been financed". The Introduction to the 1993 report compared its findings for that year with those in its report of 10 years earlier, and noted that many of the deficiencies identified in 1983 had still not been corrected.

By 1994 the Maastricht Treaty had come into effect, requiring the Court to issue a separate Statement of Assurance "as to the reliability of the accounts and the legality and regularity of the underlying transactions". The Statement for that year, as the 1994 report observed, contained "significant reservations" about the accounts' reliability, besides drawing attention, once again, to the "many errors affecting the legality and regularity" of payments. There was a welcome for a new Commission financial management improvement programme, entitled 'Sound and Efficient Management' or SEM 2000. The report for the following year, 1995, nevertheless declared that the Commission's financial management was still being criticised "in most chapters" of the report.

The Maastricht Treaty had also strengthened the powers of the Community's institutions to combat fraud, a problem which was attracting growing media attention. Within the Single Market internal customs controls had been virtually abolished, throwing greater responsibilities on controls at the external borders. In 1991 the Community had established the Matthaeus Programme for the vocational training of national customs officials, and also introduced measures for better co-ordination between them. The Court of Auditors' report for 1997 nevertheless observed caustically that after six years of Matthaeus, "a greater amount of cohesion" might have been expected.

The main losers from ineffective customs controls were of course the national exchequers rather than the EU. Failure to collect tariffs and levies on goods from outside the EU, however, reduced that element of 'traditional own resources', as did frauds on the VAT system. This provided the justification for the Court of Auditors' interest in the matter.

The main focus of the Court's 1998 report, however, continued to be deficiencies in the Commission's control of expenditure. The package of measures adopted in 1988, it observed, "seemed to represent an important turning point, promising reforms of which one of the most important was the introduction of a regime of budgetary discipline". Yet the report went on to highlight, again, "weaknesses in the accounting systems" and problems "in the operation of management and internal control systems at each level of administration, from the Commission, through intermediaries such as Member State authorities, down to the final beneficiaries".

Understanding the EU Budget

These gave rise to a

"significant number of substantive and formal errors, so that the Court again declines to give a positive statement on the legality and regularity of the transactions underlying the Commission's payments".[40]

The crisis of 1999

Throughout the 1990s, indeed, there was mounting criticism both in the media and in political circles of the way in which the Community Budget was being implemented. Investigations by the Court of Auditors and by the European Parliament's Budgetary Control Committee were revealing flagrant instances of fraud – the "pilfering on an heroic scale" referred to by the Director General of the Institute of Directors, Sir John Hoskyns, in 1989.[41] The Commission's internal systems of financial control appeared incapable of doing anything about it.

At the end of the decade matters took a dramatic turn. As the Court of Auditor's report for the year succinctly put it:

"1999 was an important year for financial management in the Community. A crisis of confidence in the Commission's management which had developed over previous years came to a head with the two reports of the Committee of Independent Experts, after the first of which the Commission resigned."[42]

In April that year, the European Parliament had reaffirmed a decision of the previous year not to grant the Commission discharge

---

40 General Introduction, para. 0.10.
41 Speech to the IoD's Annual Convention on 28 February 1989, under the title 'Why the Single Market Programme is in Trouble'.
42 General Introduction, para. 0.3.

for implementation of the 1996 Budget.[43] It recalled that there had been "an unacceptably high number of cases where the execution of the Budget has been inappropriate", and pointedly drew attention to the responsibilities of the Commissioners themselves:

> "…examples discovered during the discharge procedure have revealed a real concern that irregularities are committed without individual Commissioners perceiving the need to take personal responsibility for such actions."

Earlier, in January, Parliament had also adopted a resolution calling *inter alia* "for a committee of independent experts to be convened under the auspices of the Parliament and the Commission" to investigate "the way in which the Commission detects and deals with fraud, mismanagement and nepotism including a fundamental review of Commission practices in the awarding of all financial contracts." This committee met for the first time at the beginning of February under the chairmanship of the former Dutch President of the Court of Auditors, André Middelhoek. It worked at what, for a Community body, was exceptional speed, and produced its first report in the middle of March.[44] This turned out to be a document of explosive potential.

In accordance with its mandate from the Parliament, the Committee had left for its second report a general review of the Commission's procedures. In its first it confined itself to "giving its considered view on the question of the 'specific responsibility' of the Commission as a body and of Commissioners individually in a range of specific cases."

---

43 Report on the accounts of the European Communities in respect of the 1996 financial year. *Rapporteur* James Elles (20 April 1999 A4-0196/99, PE 230.655 final).

44 *First Report on Allegations regarding Fraud, Mismanagement and Nepotism in the European Commission* (Committee of Independent Experts, Office for Official Publications of the European Communities, 15 March 1999).

The first of these was the administration of the Community's tourism policy which had already become notorious: by 1999, "76 bodies or individuals were the subject of criminal proceedings in the Member States or of additional inquiries within the Commission". In addition, the head of the Commission's tourist office had himself been "engaging in unauthorised external activities in his sphere of responsibility, giving rise to embezzlement, corruption and favouritism." He had only been dismissed after a procedure lasting some years and on quite favourable terms. Moreover, the Commission had "failed, between April 1990 and July 1993, to take any action despite the serious warning signals constituted by the European Parliament's misgivings and the Court of Auditors' report of 30 September 1992."

The second specific case examined was the MED programme for co-operation with the countries of the Mediterranean, launched in 1992 after the Gulf War. Its budget for the period between 1992 and 1996 had been ECU 116.6m, of which about two-thirds had been committed when, in 1995, it was decided to suspend the programme. In effect, the money had been handed out to a network of private firms and consultants, without going through tendering procedures and without much attempt to discover where the money had gone. Similar problems were revealed in connection with the 'ECHO Affair': four contracts awarded in 1993 and 1994 "for the provision of humanitarian aid operations in the former Yugoslavia and in the Great Lakes region of Africa."

The Committee stated:

> "It was established during 1997/8 that these contracts were entirely fictitious, in so far as none of the activities or purchases to be financed under the alleged contracts – and indeed subsequently reported to the Commission – existed in reality."

Though it had not become notorious like tourism, MED and ECHO, the Committee also looked into the Leonardo da Vinci programme, launched in 1994 to provide finance for vocational training. Its budget for 1995–99 had been ECU 620m, the spending of which was outsourced to a 'technical assistance office': actually the French company Agenor SA. The Commission's own services had revealed a number of shortcomings in the way the money had been spent – including an "unacceptably high daily fee rates of ECU 2,677 for a professor from Exeter University" – but had failed to take the necessary prompt action.

This section of the Committee report also noted a feature of the enquiry which became an important focus of media attention – the leaking of damaging documents to the European Parliament by a whistleblower within the Commission:

> "On 26 October 1998, a few days before the debate and adoption at first reading of Parliament's resolution on the Leonardo II programme on 5 November 1998, MEPs received an anonymous 'Open letter to Members of the European Parliament' dated 26 October 1998 which closed with the demand: 'Do not vote for the proposed Leonardo da Vinci II programme at your November part-session.'"

Until the anonymous letter arrived, the *rapporteur* for Parliament's Committee on Social Affairs and Employment, the British MEP for Leicester, Sue Waddington, had received no information whatsoever about the numerous irregularities that had occurred in the implementation of the Leonardo I programme. She accordingly wrote to the President of the Commission, Jacques Santer, asking for an assurance that the allegations in the anonymous letter were false. Santer's reply, the Committee report observes, "was evasive to an extent which can only be qualified as misleading".

The Committee also examined the case of the Commission's Security Service, which had been outsourced to private Belgian companies. In 1997 the Belgian newspaper *De Morgen* had published an article criticising the contract with IMS Group 4/ Securitas, alleging in particular that Group 4's tender application in 1992 had been manipulated in order to give the company an unfair advantage in the selection process; and the employment of 'ghost' personnel. In this case, internal investigations did take place in good time, and disciplinary proceedings were initiated. The report nevertheless observed that

> "There was a peculiar complicity within the security system and between the Security Office and other circles in the Commission that created a kind of 'regulation-free-zone', where existing laws and regulations were regarded as cumbersome barriers to various forms of arbitrary action rather than as limitations to be respected."

These included such 'small favours' to colleagues in the Commission as "cancelling police fines for parking offences or drink-driving".

The Committee report also examined an area of Commission activity which had earlier attracted criticism from the Court of Auditors: irregularities in the awarding of contracts in connection with the spending of ECU 848.5m between 1990 and 1997 for nuclear safety programmes.

The affair of the Commissioner's dentist

The subject covered by the report which attracted the most media attention, however – and which probably sealed the fate of the Santer Commission – was the final one: the activities of the Commissioners themselves. The *locus classicus* was the appointment by the French Socialist Commissioner, Edith Cresson, of a personal friend, a certain M. Bertholet, as a scientific advisor. Apart from the fact that he was not qualified for the job – it was reported that he was the Commissioner's dentist – investigations had shown that he had done little work as Commission advisor, but had spent a large part of his time on paid missions to the French town of Châtellerault. The Commission's own Financial Control office had observed:

> "it was difficult not to conclude that Mr Berthelot's visiting scientist duties in 1996 and 1997 had been – primarily at least – a way of remunerating Mrs Cresson's adviser in connection with Mrs Cresson's work as mayor of Châtellerault."

A letter sent to M. Bertholet asking for details of the work he had carried out for the Commission was answered by his wife, saying that "because of the lengthy period which her husband would have to spend in hospital, she could not comply…". He had been off sick for some time (but still drawing pay).

The Committee concluded that the contracts with M. Bertholet had been illegal; and that in view of his "failure to produce even a minimum quantity of work of interest to the Commission", steps should be taken to recover the BEF 5.5m paid to him out of the Community Budget. As far as Commissioner Cresson was concerned, it concluded that "what we have here is a clear-cut case of favouritism".

Compared to the Cresson case, those raised against the other Commissioners were small beer. Commissioner Liikanen, whose wife had signed two contracts with the Commission, was cleared of all blame. Commissioner Marin's wife had actually got a job at the Commission, but there had been no irregularity. The same was true of Commissioner Pinheiro's wife (a professor at the University of Minho). Allegations against the Commission President in the Luxembourg press were held to be unfounded. Finally, Commissioner Wulf-Mathies, in a case similar to that of Commissioner Cresson, had appointed the husband of a friend as a legal expert, but at least he had been a qualified lawyer and genuinely worked for the Commission (though the report found that the procedures had "bordered on the inappropriate"). The

Committee's report therefore effectively exonerated all the individual Commissioners apart from Mme Cresson.

Its verdict on the Commission as a collective body, however, was damning. The Commissioners had claimed that they had not known about the various cases of fraud and corruption. However,

> "protestations of ignorance on the part of Commissioners concerning problems that were often common knowledge in their services, even up to the highest official levels, are tantamount to an admission of a loss of control by the political authorities over the Administration that they are supposedly running."

The report concluded with severe criticism of the Commission's internal financial control procedures; and also with a much-quoted final paragraph containing the charge that, within the Commission, "it is becoming difficult to find anyone who has even the slightest sense of responsibility". Possibly taking this to heart, the entire Commission resigned. Had it not done so it is virtually certain that it would have been dismissed by the European Parliament.

21st century reforms

The Committee's second report,[45] an "analysis of current practice and proposals for tackling mismanagement, irregularities and fraud", was published in September 1999, and contained 90 recommendations for improving the Commission's budgetary role. These covered, first, the Commission's procedures for awarding contracts and subsidies: the annual number of contracts (including those for external aid) came at the time to roughly 11,200 with a value of €4bn; and nearly 7,000 commitments related to subsidies,

---

45 *Second Report on Reform of the Commission: Analysis of current practice and proposals for tackling mismanagement, irregularities and fraud* (Office for Official Publications of the European Communities, 10 September 1999).

totalling over another €1bn. (The difference between a contract and a subsidy, the report stated, was "extremely debatable, both in theory and in practice".)

The report also outlined suggestions for a radical shake-up of internal financial controls; and there were a number of recommendations for improving the Commission's internal staffing and recruitment procedures. Among these were the revolutionary suggestions that appointments and promotions should be based more on merit than on nationality, and that more should be done to penalise manifest incompetence. The accountability of the Commission to the European Parliament was also stressed. In a clear reference to the revelations contained in the first report it advised that

> "any Commissioner who knowingly misleads Parliament, or omits to correct at the earliest opportunity inadvertently erroneous information provided to Parliament, should be expected to offer his/her resignation from the Commission. In the absence of an offer of resignation, the President of the Commission should take appropriate action."

The bulk of the report, however, was a detailed analysis of the problems faced by the Commission in exercising proper control over expenditure, particularly when its responsibilities were shared with the national administrations, as in the cases of the CAP and the Regional and Social Funds: i.e. about 80% of the total. (The problems arising from this situation are examined more extensively in Chapter 5). As far as the Commission's own internal systems were concerned, the report painted a bleak picture of misallocated staff, confusing rules and procedures, lack of co-ordination and – as emphasised in the first report – no clear picture of where the buck stopped in the event of errors. Expenditure under the heading 'co-operation with non-member countries', for example, was a "self-contained, chaotic area, given the numerous and diverse legal rules by which it is governed".

A "professional and independent Internal Audit service" was needed; and authorising officers needed to "be responsible, consider themselves responsible and held responsible".

The criticisms of the Commission's administration of the Budget during the 1990s had, in fact, already produced some reforms, even before the publication of the Committee's reports. One of these was the establishment in 1999 of an independent European Anti-Fraud Office (OLAF). It was not an entirely new concept: it replaced the 'Task Force for the Co-ordination of fraud prevention' (UCLAF) which had been part of the Secretariat-General of the Commission since 1988. OLAF, however, was given greater powers of independent investigation, and was tasked, in particular, with fighting frauds carried out by transnational organised crime.

There was nevertheless some criticism of the basis on which OLAF had been set up. Although declared to be independent, it was, like its predecessor, established within the institutional structure of the Commission, and answerable to the Commissioner with responsibility for taxation. On the other hand, the Office was made subject to regular control by a Supervisory Committee, made up of five qualified outside persons independent of the Community's institutions. The appointment of OLAF's Director-General was also made subject to this Committee's approval; and, following appointment, he or she was placed under an obligation (similar to that of ECB governors) "neither to seek nor take instructions from any government or any institution", including the Commission itself.

One important recommendation of the Committee of Independent Experts' second report was that the Financial Regulation – the document laying down the procedures for drawing up, adopting and implementing the Budget – was in urgent need of reform. Throughout the 1980s and 1990s the Community had been operating on the basis of a Regulation adopted at the end of 1977, although the scope and scale of the Budget and the activities it financed had considerably expanded. Accordingly, a reformed Financial Regulation for what had now become the European Union was adopted in June 2002. This was intended to "satisfy the need for rigour and a simpler legislative and administrative set-up", and was supplemented by detailed technical rules for its implementation.

The Berlin Council of March 1999, in addition to agreeing a five-year financial perspective for 2000–2006, had also made a number of other changes in the budgetary field. The percentage of so-called 'traditional' own resources (i.e. customs duties and sugar levies) retained by Member States to cover collection costs was increased from 10% to 25%; new rules were put in place for financing the UK rebate: the contributions of Austria, Germany, the Netherlands and Sweden were cut to 25% of the normal rate; and certain 'windfall' gains for the UK – made as a result of, for example, enlargement – were 'neutralised'. In 2005 further adjustments were made, designed to reduce the UK rebate, to be phased in between 2009 and 2011. The total loss to the UK was, however, capped at €10.5bn in 2004 prices. In 2010 the UK's net budgetary contribution was estimated to be just over €10bn.

Meanwhile, within the Commission itself, one of the survivors from the Santer Commission, the British Commissioner Neil Kinnock, was given the job of correcting some of the organisational defects highlighted by the Experts. Yet he was soon embroiled in the 'Andreassen affair'. In 2002 a Spanish official, Marta Andreassen, was brought in as the Commission's chief accountant as part of the clear-up programme. Shortly afterwards, she submitted an internal report describing the accounting systems she found as "chaotic"; but then, unsatisfied with the response from the Commissioners – in particular Kinnock and the new President, Romano Prodi – she went public. She was at first suspended and eventually, in 2004, she was sacked, leading to charges in the European Parliament that she had been made a scapegoat for a lack of progress in reform.

In 2009 (after Kinnock had left the Commission) Andreassen was elected as a United Kingdom Independence Party (UKIP) Member of the European Parliament for the South East Region of England. In this she was following in the footsteps of an earlier whistleblower, the Dutch official Paul van Buitenen, who was responsible for providing much of the information leading to the appointment of the Committee of Independent Experts. After resigning as a Commission official in 2002, van Buitenen was two years later elected as a Dutch MEP – also having become a Knight of the Order of Orange-Nassau.

Positive indicators

The crisis of 1999 and its outcome, however, did produce some marked improvements in the management of the EU Budget. The Introduction to the Court of Auditors' report for 2000, unusually, includes a section headed 'There are some positive findings':

"... For example, in the agricultural area the reformed clearance-of-accounts system and the integrated administrative and control system have contributed to improved, if not yet fully satisfactory, management of large amounts of EU funds, and the milk quota regime has restricted production to the target level. The Commission's strategy for dealing with BSE is basically sound. With regard to structural measures, the URBAN Community initiative has helped the implementation of many urban development projects and has enabled local authorities to access European Union funds. In the external actions area the work of the Agency charged with the reconstruction of Kosovo was both efficient and economical. The Tacis cross-border co-operation programme is an instrument which has the potential to play a useful role in addressing issues relating to the new eastern border following the next accession."

The outturn of the 2000 Budget, however, also featured the largest surplus of revenue over expenditure ever recorded: €11.6bn, or 14% of payments. Both VAT and customs duties had produced more revenue than forecast, largely because the EU's rate of economic growth had been underestimated. What might in national budgetary terms have been a happy event, however, did not secure the approval of the Court: carrying forward large sums to the following year would "significantly distort" that year's revenue position. In the absence of better forecasting, the money should have been returned to the Member States via an amending or supplementary budget.

By 2001 the reforms advocated by the Experts in 1999 were well under way. The Court of Auditors' report for the year observes that the Commission had "taken important steps to clarify responsibility and accountability for the management of Community funds" and had "shown its commitment to build on the results of this first year by presenting an 18-point action plan to address the weaknesses identified."[46] A new Financial Regulation was in place, and would come into effect for the following year's Budget. On the other hand, the budget surplus for the year was even greater than in 2000: 16% of payments.

In 2004, the number of EU Member States rose, all at once, from 15 to 25. The 2004 Budget, originally adopted on the basis of the original 15, had therefore to be changed by an amending budget in March of that year, with commitments and payments rising by 11.5% and 7.8% respectively over 2003 (though this turned out to be an over-estimate of the funds that could eventually be spent). Uncertainties as to the actual financial impact of enlargement resulted in no fewer than eight amending budgets during 2005, the overall effect of which was a reduction rather

---

46 General Introduction, para. 0.13.

than an increase in spending. Overall commitments, however, rose substantially.

Meanwhile, the Commission continued to implement reforms to its systems of financial control, with substantial changes to its accounting systems coming into effect in 2005. In 2006 the Commission adopted two reports outlining progress in improving internal financial controls;[47] and also an action plan for an 'integrated internal control framework'.[48] The Court of Auditors welcomed the progress, while urging the Commission to "continue its efforts".

The Court of Auditors' reports for the first decade of the 21st century, indeed, provide a marked contrast to those of earlier years. The aura of Commission/Court antagonism had gone. The report for 2009 estimated that the error rate on payments lay between 2% and 5%, and concluded mildly that "the supervisory and control systems for payments are in general partially effective." Only in the case of the €35.5bn Cohesion Fund (admittedly a sizable portion of the Budget) were supervisory and control systems considered to be "not effective". Moreover, the Court found "a continuing reduction in the most likely error rate…for payments as a whole over recent years".

---

47 COM(2007) 67 of 28.2.2007 and COM(2007) 274 of 30.5.2007
48 COM(2006) 9 of 17.1.2006

Chapter 3

How the Budget is decided

Searching finance

The Lisbon Treaty

The reports of the Committee of Independent Experts had charted a way through the problems connected with the *implementation* of the Budget, and in particular the tensions between the Commission on the one hand and the Parliament and the Court of Auditors on the other. There remained, however, problems connected to the *adoption* of the Budget, and the tensions between the two wings of the 'budgetary authority': Council and Parliament.

The European Parliament's role in adopting general Community legislation had been steadily increasing as a result of the Single European Act adopted in 1986 and the Maastricht Treaty of 1992. As far as the treaties went, however, the budgetary procedures had remained much as they had been in the late 1970s. Instead, there had been a mass of implementing Regulations and significant *ad hoc* arrangements: notably the Inter-Institutional Agreement of 1988 and subsequent IIAs, under which multiannual financial frameworks (MFFs) were adopted. The Agreements also set out how these multiannual programmes were to be managed on a year-to-year basis: for example, the procedures for revisions and adjustments. Each year, a whole series of technical issues needed to be agreed between the two budgetary wings: the classification of expenditure, the provision of a legal base for financial provisions, the 'maximum rate of increase' for expenditure, both in detail and in aggregate, and so on.

As far as the treaty framework was concerned, major changes were eventually made by the Lisbon Treaty of 2007. The procedures for adopting MFFs for periods of at least five years were formalised, and the European Parliament at last achieved the same powers over budgetary lines which had once been classified as 'compulsory' as over the rest.

Revision of the budgetary procedure

The budgetary procedure established by Article 272 of the Lisbon Treaty roughly follows the pattern first adopted in the ECSC in 1952. The stages are:

1   By 1 July of the preceding year each EU organisation, including all those not formally described as 'institutions', but excluding the independent ECB, draw up their estimates for the following year.

2   The Commission consolidates these estimates into a draft budget, containing estimates of both expenditure and revenue. This must be submitted to the Council and the Parliament by 1 September at the latest. The Commission can, however, amend its draft any time before the start of stage 5 below.

3   The Council adopts its position on the draft budget, including any amendments, and passes it to the Parliament before 1 October.

4   Within 42 days, Parliament must either adopt the Budget as it stands – in practice this will occur at a 'first reading' plenary sitting in October – or amend it "by a majority of its component members" and send it back to Council. If it does nothing, the Budget is "deemed to have been adopted".

5   Within 10 days, the Council can accept Parliament's amendments. If it does not, a joint Council/Parliament Conciliation Committee is convened. This Committee is tasked with agreeing a joint text within 21 days, with the Commission participating in order to broker an agreement. If the conciliation procedure fails, the Commission must propose a new draft budget.

6   If a joint text *is* agreed by the Conciliation Committee, Council and Parliament have 14 days to approve or reject it. If one approves and the other fails to take a decision, or both fail to take a decision, the Budget is "deemed to be definitively adopted in accordance with the joint text".

7   Even if Council rejects the joint text, Parliament may re-confirm some or all of its earlier amendments, and adopt the Budget, acting by "a majority of its component members and three-fifths of the votes cast".

8   If Council and Parliament both reject the joint text, or Parliament rejects the text "by a majority of its component members" while Council approves it, the Budget is rejected and the Commission has to submit a new draft.

9   If, at the beginning of a financial year – that is, 1 January – the Budget has not been definitively adopted, the system of twelfths comes into operation. A sum equivalent to one-twelfth of the budget appropriations for the preceding financial year may be spent each month. Meanwhile, Commission, Council and Parliament try to agree a Budget for the year.

10   Once the budgetary procedure has, at any stage, been successfully completed, the Budget is "definitively adopted" through a declaration by Parliament's President.

Figure 3.1: The budgetary procedure in 2011

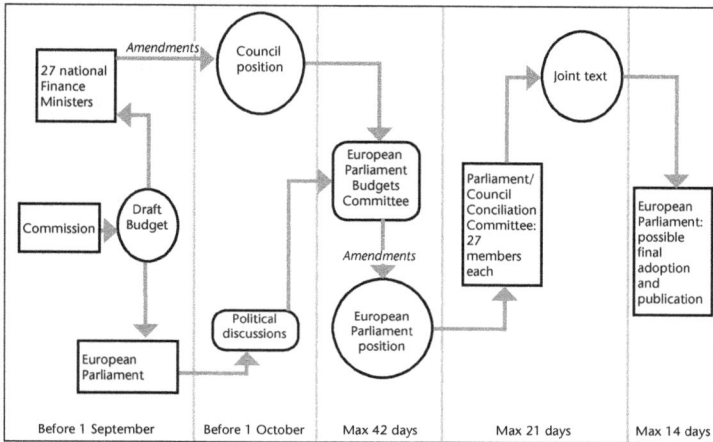

Source: EU Commission

This procedure may seem complex; but it is a great deal simpler than that which was used in earlier years, when different procedures applied to 'administrative' and 'operational' items, or to 'compulsory' and 'non-compulsory' expenditure. The confusing distinction between 'amendments' and 'modifications' has gone, as have the different majorities necessary in Parliament and Council to adopt them. There is still a distinction between expenditure "necessarily resulting from this Treaty or from acts adopted in accordance therewith", and the rest, to which a "maximum rate of increase" continues to apply. The Commission fixes this on the basis of:

◆ The trend, in terms of volume, of the gross national product within the Community;

◆ The average variation in the budgets of the Member States; and

◆ The trend of the cost of living during the preceding financial year.

No representation without taxation?

Compared to earlier procedures, Lisbon significantly tipped the balance of budgetary power between Parliament and Council in favour of the Parliament – at least as far as the annual budgetary procedure is concerned. Whether, in practice, this is a good or bad development is a matter of opinion. In the past, Parliament has usually supported the Commission in voting for higher expenditure, whereas the Council has generally tried to impose budgetary restraint. In some respects, indeed, the Parliament has acted in a way very similar to that of the US Congress, with Members voting for projects favouring the States from which they come (e.g. higher agricultural spending) or their political ideology (e.g. environmental projects). Negotiations between political and national groups within the Parliament, on the basis of *quid pro quo*, have ensured that many of these obtain the necessary parliamentary majorities.

A second reason for the situation, however, lies in a fundamental difference between the procedure for adopting the EU Budget and those that apply in Member States. The European Parliament has the power to vote expenditure; but it does not have to vote directly on the taxes necessary to fund it. By contrast, the governments represented in the Council, and the national parliaments that support them, have to find the overwhelming bulk of the revenue to pay for EU spending. In this sense the concept of 'own resources' is a fraud.

This is something which has been obvious for some time. As the study *Stable Money – Sound Finances*, already quoted, observed in 1993:

> "A situation in which the budget is overwhelmingly funded by national contributions is politically unsatisfactory in the longer term…. The EC budget threatens then to be much

more a function of national budgetary priorities than the concern of the Community and its citizens. Because national contributions are not always perceived by Member State governments and parliaments as genuine EC own resources, there is great reluctance to raise the budget....."[49]

The study concluded that the situation in fact constituted an argument for the creation of genuine EU taxes of the kind outlined in Chapter 1. If the European Parliament, in addition to voting on the expenditure side of the Budget, had also to vote on the rates of a 'federal' VAT or a 'federal' corporation tax to fund it, its behaviour might be very different. At the same time the Council would no longer have to be constantly looking over its collective shoulder at the reaction of its national parliaments and taxpayers. The blame for any tax rises would lie clearly with the European Parliament.

The apparent increase in Parliament's budgetary powers contained in the Lisbon Treaty, however, is not all that it seems. The decision to establish five- to seven-year MFFs, now enshrined in the Treaty, has considerably reduced the room for manoeuvre in establishing annual Budgets. Accordingly, the forum for conflict between Council and Parliament has shifted from the annual procedures to those establishing the multiannual frameworks.

This change has not been lost on the Parliament – its decision to hold up adoption of the 2011 Budget was not so much because it objected to the Budget itself, but in order to obtain a bargaining counter in the impending negotiations for the 2014–2020 framework.

Amendments and transfers

It might be thought that, once an annual Budget has been adopted, that is the end of the matter until the following year. As mentioned in the Introduction to this book, however, that can

---

[49] *op. cit.* p.82.

be far from the case. In the event of "unavoidable, exceptional or unforeseen circumstances", the Commission may propose during the year that the Budget as adopted be amended. This it does by submitting 'draft amending budgets', which have to be adopted by the same procedures as the general Budget itself. There were seven of these in 2010.

One use of amending budgets is to enter balances from the previous year in the Budget for the current year. This frequently arises because sums entered for payment that year, for a variety of reasons, cannot in the end be spent. Yet, as the very first full-year report of the Court of Auditors pointed out in 1979,

> "the under-utilisation of payment appropriations... is a very serious matter since it calls into question both the basis on which the budgetary estimates were drawn up and the soundness of the financial management".

Part of the problem at the time, it noted, was the "practice of including in the budget provision for policies which have yet to be launched". The accounts for 1978 had also shown no less than a 50% under-spend in the cases of the CAP guidance section and the Regional and Social Funds (i.e. what became the Structural Funds) and the appropriations for energy and research. The Court recognised that the fault did not lie wholly with the Commission: part was attributable to "slowness on the part of the Member States in submitting satisfactory claims for payment". Nevertheless, experience should have led to "more realistic estimates". Yet over 30 years later, the problem of under-spend has not gone away, as the quotation from the *Financial Times* of 10 November 2010 in Chapter 1 indicates.

Supplementary budgets, carryovers (the spending of which must take place within time-rules established in the Financial Regulation) and transfers are often, therefore, elements of sensible financial management; the decision in 1988 to enclose the annual Budgets within an agreed five- or seven-year Financial

Perspective, according to some,[50] risked placing them in an inflexible straightjacket. Each budget heading has its own ceiling, and the broad pattern of spending is notionally fixed for the duration of the agreement. This problem has indeed been recognised by the Commission, which observed in its 2010 Budget Review:[51]

> "Since their introduction in 1988, the EU's multiannual financial frameworks have ensured strict budgetary discipline and medium-term predictability of EU expenditure. This predictability has come at the price of limited flexibility. The past years have shown that the financial framework and its programmes have not always been able to respond to political imperatives and changing circumstances."

In practice, the frameworks have proved reasonably malleable. On 19 September 2007, for example, the Commission proposed a revision to provide an additional €309m for the European Institute of Technology (EIT), and an additional €2.4bn for Galileo, the European Navigation Satellite System programme, following the failure of negotiations with a private consortium. Appropriate amendments to the budgetary framework were agreed by Parliament and Council at the end of that year.

These substantial new projects were nevertheless controversial for another reason: their funding was made possible as a result of substantial under-spending on agricultural support, and on cohesion funding. In principle, these surpluses should have been credited back to the Member States (see next Chapter).

The extent to which unspent appropriations can be reallocated to entirely new projects (as opposed to being transferred to existing budgetary lines or carried over in accordance with the Financial Regulation) is now an issue of contention as the negotiations begin on the 2014–2020 Financial Perspective.

---

[50] See, for example, Professor Iain Begg in *Funding the European Union* (Federal Trust, March 2005).

[51] *op.cit.*

Chapter 4

The structure of the Budget

Searching finance

Anyone wishing to follow in detail the inception, adoption and implementation of an EU budget needs space for a considerable number of documents – although it is true that all these can now be accessed electronically.

The financial framework

Following the Inter-Institutional Agreement of 1988, each annual Budget has first to be seen in the context of the relevant MFF. Currently, this is the framework agreed in 2006 to cover the years 2007 to 2013 (see Table 4.2).

One complicating factor, however, is the need for 'technical adjustments' each year to update the figures contained in the original framework. These adjustments, carried out by the Commission, are of two kinds:

1   The MFF is drawn up at constant prices. As a result, the figures have to be revised to take account of inflation, so ensuring that each expenditure heading has constant purchasing power.

2   The ceiling on own resources is expressed as a percentage of Gross National Income (GNI). Translating this ceiling into an absolute figure involves new calculations each year on the basis of the most recent GNI data.[52]

The framework can also be changed from year to year for other reasons. The Commission can propose, for example:

◆   A rescheduling of payment appropriations available for structural operations where delays have been identified in the programming of such operations; and

◆   Revisions as a result of the accession of new Member States.

---

52 This is carried out via a methodology laid down in Council Regulation (EC, Euratom) No 1287/2003 of 15 July 2003 on the harmonisation of gross national income at market prices (GNI Regulation).

In addition, as noted earlier, Council and Parliament can revise the framework to fund projects or actions not foreseen at the time the framework was drawn up. They can depart by up to 5% from the financial envelope set in the legislative acts for multiannual programmes over the life of the programme concerned – or more if new, objective, long-term circumstances arise. Upward revisions of the ceilings can be made to meet unforeseen circumstances, with the possibility of lowering other ceilings to compensate.[53]

Outside the formal structure of the financial framework there are also a number of contingency funds (see Table 4.1):

◆ An *emergency aid reserve*, fixed at €221m a year for the duration of the framework, enables the EU to provide aid to third (i.e. non-member) countries following events which could not be foreseen when a budget was established;

◆ A €1bn *Solidarity Fund*, established in 2002,[54] allows swift financial assistance in the event of major disasters occurring on the territory of a Member State or of a candidate country;[55]

◆ The *flexibility instrument*, with an annual ceiling of €200m, is intended to allow clearly identified expenditure which could not be financed within the limits of the heading ceilings available; and

---

53 Details of how these possibilities for revision have been used can be found in *Flexibility in the Multiannual Financial Framework 2007 – 2013: revisions and use of instruments* (European Parliament Directorate-General for Internal Policies, October 2010).

54 See Council Regulation (EC) No 2012/2002 of 11 November 2002.

55 A natural disaster is considered as 'major' if:

• In the case of a State, it results in damage estimated either at over €3bn in 2002 prices), or at more than 0.6% of its gross national income;

• By way of exception, the Fund may be mobilised for extraordinary regional disasters resulting in damage below this threshold, affecting the major part of its population, with serious and lasting repercussions on living conditions and the economic stability of the region.

- ◆ Finally, a *Globalisation Adjustment Fund* of €500m maximum a year is intended to provide additional support for workers who suffer from the consequences of major structural changes in world trade patterns.

Between 2007 and 2010 over €3bn was spent under these flexibility instruments.

Table 4.1: Use of flexibility instruments (€m)

	2007	2008	2009	2010	2007–10
Emergency Aid Reserve	49	422	188	232	891
European Union Solidarity Fund	197	273	623	80	1,172
Flexibility Instrument	0	270	420	213	903
European Globalisation Adjustment Fund	19	49	52	63	182
Total flexibility instruments	**264**	**1,014**	**1,283**	**588**	**3,149**

Source: European Parliament

The Financial Regulation: budgetary principles

The basic principles governing the form of the Budget, and also the rules for its implementation, are contained in the Financial Regulation, and in the legislation laying down the detailed rules for the Regulation's application. Those currently in force were adopted in June 2002,[56] and replaced the Regulation of December 1977. The detailed technical arrangements – CommissionRegulation (EC, EURATOM) No 2342/2002[57] – were adopted in December of 2002, replacing those adopted in 1993.

---

[56] *Council Regulation (EC, Euratom) No 1605/2002 on the Financial Regulation applicable to the general budget of the European Communities* (OJ L 357, 31.12.2002, OJ L 248, 16.9.2002, p.1).

[57] *Commission Regulation (EC, EURATOM) No 2342/2002 of 23 December 2002 laying down detailed rules for the implementation of Council Regulation (EC, Euratom) No 1605/2002 on the Financial Regulation applicable to the general budget of the European Communities* (OJ L 357, 31.12.2002,OJ L 248, 16.9.2002, p.1).

The new Regulation is simpler than the old, and is largely confined to reaffirming and clarifying a number of "basic principles and definitions relating to the establishment, execution and control" of the Budget which are laid down in the treaties.

The principle of unity

All revenue and expenditure must be entered in the Budget – a principle which may seem obvious, but clarifies the status, for example, of such recondite sums as interest on pre-financing payments, the "proceeds of sanctions imposed on Member States declared to have an excessive deficit" (if ever that were to occur!) and "charges entailed by acceptance of donations to the Communities". EU expenditure now includes the operational expenditure relating to the common foreign and security policy, and on police and judicial cooperation in criminal matters, where these are charged to the Budget.

The principle of annuality

Expenditure entered in the Budget is authorised for one financial year only, which runs from 1 January to 31 December. Commitments to spend, however, can be made to run over several years; in certain circumstances, unspent appropriations can be carried over to subsequent years (see later sections of this Chapter).

The principle of equilibrium

Budget revenues and budget payment appropriations must be in balance – as noted in Chapter 1, the EU is not authorised to raise loans in order to cover its expenditure. Any balance from a financial year is entered in the Budget for the following financial year as revenue in the case of a surplus, or as a payment appropriation in the case of a deficit.

Table 4.2: The financial framework 2007–2013

Commitment appropriations (€m, 2004 prices)	2007	2008	2009	2010	2011	2012	2013	Total 2007–2013
Sustainable growth	51 267	52 913	54 071	54 860	55 379	56 845	58 256	383 591
1a. Competitiveness for growth and employment	8 404	9 595	10 209	11 000	11 306	12 122	12 914	75 550
1b. Cohesion for growth and employment	42 863	43 318	43 862	43 860	44 073	44 723	45 342	308 041
2.Preservation and Management of Natural Resources	53 478	54 322	53 666	53 035	52 400	51 775	51 161	369 837
of which: market-related expenditure and direct payments	43 120	42 697	42 279	41 864	41 453	41 047	40 645	293 105
Citizenship, Freedom, Security and Justice	1 199	1 258	1 380	1 503	1 645	1 797	1 988	10 770
3a. Freedom, Security and Justice	600	690	790	910	1 050	1 200	1 390	6 630
3b. Citizenship	599	568	590	593	595	597	598	4 140
4.The EU as a global player	6 199	6 469	6 739	7 009	7 339	7 679	8 029	49 463
5. Administration	6 633	6 818	6 973	7 111	7 255	7 400	7 610	49 800
6. Compensations	419	191	190	-	-	-	-	800
Total appropriations for commitments	119 195	121 971	123 019	123 518	124 018	125 496	127 044	864 261
as a percentage of GNI	1.10 %	1.08 %	1.07 %	1.04 %	1.03 %	1.02 %	1.01 %	1.048 %
Total appropriations for payments	115 142	119 805	112 182	118 549	116 178	119 659	119 161	820 676
as a percentage of GNI	1.06 %	1.06 %	0.97 %	1.00 %	0.97 %	0.97 %	0.94 %	1.00 %
Margin available	0.18 %	0.18 %	0.27 %	0.24 %	0.27 %	0.27 %	0.29 %	0.24 %
Own Resources Ceiling as a percentage of GNI	1.24 %	1.24 %	1.24 %	1.24 %	1.24 %	1.24 %	1.24 %	1.24 %

Notes to Table 4.2:
The figures given in the financial framework are annual ceilings for each expenditure category under the general budget of the EU. For each of the years covered by the financial framework, total required payment appropriations must not be such as to produce a call-in rate for own resources that exceeds the own resources ceiling.

Subtitle 1(a) (Competitiveness for growth and employment) covers activities which aim to strengthen the EU's growth potential, such as research, education and trans-European networks.

Subtitle 1(b) (Cohesion for growth and employment) aims to improve growth and prosperity throughout the EU.

Title 2 puts together a comprehensive approach to the EU's natural resources, including agriculture (market expenditure and direct allocations), rural development, fishing and the environment.

Subtitle 3(a) (Freedom, security and justice) includes activities with a view to strengthening fundamental rights, stepping up the fight against terrorism and organised crime, and addressing the issues of immigration and judicial co-operation.

Subtitle 3(b) (Citizenship) covers activities promoting European culture, protecting public health and fostering solidarity within the EU.

Title 4 covers EU activities outside of its borders, including enlargement, bilateral relations, regional-level relations with its neighbours, humanitarian aid and development aid.

Source: EU Commission

The principle of unit of account

Since coming into existence in 1999, the euro has been the unit of account for drawing up and implementing the Community Budget and presenting the accounts. However, in practice certain operations are carried out in national currencies – where these still exist – subject to conditions laid down in the rules for the implementation of the Financial Regulation: for example, the exchange rates to be used.

The principle of universality

Total budget revenue covers total budget expenditure – revenue cannot be 'hypothecated' for spending on specific items. Some exceptions are allowed: for example, Member States' financial contributions to certain research programmes and contributions from third countries to the Community's activities in the framework of the European Economic Area (EEA). Linked to this principle is the 'no-offsetting' rule: revenue and expenditure cannot be netted off against each other, the only exceptions again being those specifically authorised by the Regulation or the implementing rules.

The principle of specification

Each appropriation must be earmarked for a specific purpose and assigned to a specific item of expenditure. For this reason the Budget is divided, and subdivided, into its hierarchy of sections, titles, chapters, articles and items. Again, application of the principle can be modified by allowing transfers between budgetary lines (see later in this Chapter).

The principle of sound financial management

This is another principle which might seem obvious, but which history, as recorded by the Court of Auditors, shows to have been frequently breached. In operational terms, application of the

principle entails defining verifiable objectives which are monitored
– *ex ante*; interim; and *ex post* – using measurable performance
indicators. For example, the *ex ante* evaluations under the rules
implementing the Financial Regulation, should indicate:

"(a) the need to be met in the short- or long-term;

(b) the added value of Community involvement;

(c) the objectives to be achieved;

(d) the policy options available, including the risks associated
with them;

(e) the results and impacts expected, in particular economic,
social and environmental impacts, and the indicators and
evaluation arrangement needed to measure them;

(f) the most appropriate method of implementation for the
preferred option(s);

(g) the internal coherence of the proposed programme or activity and its relations with other relevant instruments;

(h) the volume of appropriations, human resources and other
administrative expenditure to be allocated with due regard
for the cost effectiveness principle; and

(i) the lessons learned from similar experiences in the past."

The principle of transparency

Not only the Budget, but as far as possible the decisions and
reasoning behind it, should be open to scrutiny. Annual budgets and amending budgets are published in the *Official Journal*
of the European Union two months following their adoption by
the Parliament. The Financial Regulation and its implementing
rules indicate what information must be included and the form
in which it is presented. For example, the summary statement of
revenue and expenditure in the Budget should show the estimated
revenue for the financial year in question; the estimated revenue

for the preceding financial year and the revenue for year n-2; the commitment and payment appropriations for the financial year in question and the preceding financial year; the expenditure committed and the expenditure paid in year n-2; a summary statement of the schedule of payments due in subsequent financial years; and appropriate remarks on each subdivision. The Budget also contains an establishment plan for each section of the Budget and shows borrowing and lending operations.

One further essential feature of the budget, which might also qualify as a basic principle, is that laid down in Article 268 of the Treaty.

> "The implementation of expenditure shown in the budget shall require the prior adoption of a legally binding Union act providing a legal basis for its action and for the implementation of the corresponding expenditure in accordance with the regulation referred to in Article 279, except in cases for which that law provides."

As the earlier Court of Auditors' reports observed, one reason for failure to spend appropriations included in the Budget was that the necessary legal base for the relevant action had not been previously adopted. The circumstances in which appropriations can appear and be spent *without* a prior basic act have therefore required careful definition. Among such exceptions listed by Financial Regulation are:

- Appropriations for pilot schemes of an experimental nature, designed to test the feasibility of an action and its usefulness;
- Appropriations for preparatory studies or activities with a view to providing the justification and legal base for future action;
- Appropriations for one-off actions, or even actions for an indefinite duration, for the implementation of which the Commission has specific authority; and

- ◆ Appropriations for the operation of each institution under its administrative autonomy.

In all other cases the 'remarks' column of the Budget should include a reference to the basic act giving rise to the appropriation.

The annual Budget

Within the multiannual framework, and structured according to the Financial Regulation and the regulations implementing it, the establishment of each annual Budget can then be tracked via a succession of preliminary documents. These include:

- ◆ The estimates of the institutions, available in the early months of the preceding year;
- ◆ Working documents of the Commission and other institutions, and reports adopted by the European Parliament, outlining the policies and priorities behind the Budget;
- ◆ The consolidated draft budget prepared by the Commission, usually available in the early summer, but at the latest at the beginning of September;
- ◆ The position of the Council, available before the end of September;
- ◆ The draft reports of the European Parliament's Budgets Committee, and the opinions submitted to it by all the Committees responsible for the various policies funded by the Budget (Agriculture, Regions, Social, etc.);
- ◆ Parliament's initial position voted at its budget plenary in October;
- ◆ The texts arising from any Council/Parliament conciliation procedure; and
- ◆ The reports, speeches and Budget texts as adopted – if the Budget is adopted – at Parliament's December plenary.

The adopted Budget will then be published in two volumes, in the 23 EU official languages.

Volume I provides a detailed statement of EU budget revenue as well as the revenue and expenditure of each of the institutions, apart from the Commission. These sections, covering administrative expenditure, are:

I   The European Parliament;
II   The Council;
IV   The European Court of Justice;
V   The Court of Auditors;
VI   The Economic and Social Committee;
VII   The Committee of the Regions;
VIII   The Ombudsman;
IX   The Data-Protection Supervisor; and
X   The European External Action Service.

The missing Section III – in fact the main part of the Budget – appears in Volume II and covers all the revenue and expenditure linked to EU policies. Since 2004, the structure of this section has been 'activity based' (described as ABB, short for activity-based budgeting): the Budget is divided into some 30 policy areas, each of which is described within a title (T). Titles are broken down into chapters (each corresponding to an activity), which in turn may be broken down into articles; and those in turn, where necessary, into items. The ABB nomenclature is complemented by defining each Budget article or item according to the headings of the financial framework.

Also included in the Budget is the spending of the 30 EU autonomous agencies and executive agencies; and also of the 13 European Schools.[58] The former – most of which have been created during the last 10 years – spend some €1.5bn a year (see Table 4.3).The latter – which together have over 22,000 pupils, mostly the children of EU staff – have a budget of over €250m.

---

[58] Five of these are in Belgium (four in Brussels), three in Germany, two in Luxembourg, and there is one each in Italy, Spain, the Netherlands and the UK. The UK school is at Culham, in Oxfordshire.

Table 4.3: The agencies – location and budget (payments) in 2009

Agency	Location	€m
EURATOM Supply Agency (ESA)	Luxembourg	*
European Centre for the Development of Vocational Training	Thessaloniki	18.6
European Foundation for the Improvement of Living and Working Conditions	Dublin	20.2
European Environment Agency	Copenhagen	39.8
European Training Foundation	Turin	21.8
European Monitoring Centre for Drugs and Drug Addiction	Lisbon	14.7
European Medicines Agency	London	194.4
Translation Centre for the Bodies of the European Union	Luxembourg	62.6
Community Plant Variety Office	Angers	13.2
Office for Harmonisation in the Internal Market	Alicante	338.1
European Agency for Safety and Health at Work	Bilbao	15.0
European Fundamental Rights Agency	Vienna	17.2
European Police College	Bramshill	8.8
Eurojust	The Hague	27.6
European Aviation Safety Agency	Cologne	122.0
European Maritime Safety Agency	Lisbon	53.3
European Food Safety Authority	Parma	71.0
European Network and Information Security Agency	Heraklion	8.1
European Railway Agency	Valenciennes	21.0
European Centre for Disease Prevention and Control	Stockholm	49.3
European Agency for the Management of Operational Cooperation at the External Border	Warsaw	88.8
European GNSS Supervisory Authority	Brussels	44.4
Community Fisheries Control Agency	Vigo	10.1
European Chemicals Agency	Helsinki	70.4
Executive Agency for Competitiveness and Innovation	Brussels	13.3
Education, Audiovisual and Culture Executive Agency	Brussels	47.7
Executive Agency for Health and Consumers	Luxembourg	64.0
Trans-European Transport Network Executive Agency	Brussels	8.9
Research Executive Agency	Brussels	21.6
European Research Council Executive Agency	Brussels	14.5
Total		**1,500.6**

Note: * The funding of the ESA, which has been in existence since 1960, is currently in dispute. The Court of Auditors observed in its 2009 report that "with regard to the EURATOM Supply Agency, the Court draws attention to the fact that in contradiction to its Statutes, the Agency had no budget for the year 2009 and consequently all the Agency's expenditure, except for the bank charges, was paid by the Commission." The Commission, in turn, commented that "when preparing the 2008 budget, the Commission proposed a budget for the EURATOM Supply Agency (ESA). This was refused by the Budgetary Authority and so the Commission took charge of all the expenses incurred by the ESA in 2008. The Commission continued to take charge of the ESA's expenses in the 2009 and 2010 budgets and has proposed to do likewise for 2011."

Source: European Court of Auditors' Report, 2009

Differentiation, commitments and payments

A feature of the EU Budget which can cause confusion is the classification of items as 'differentiated' or 'non-differentiated' appropriations.

Non-differentiated appropriations are straightforward: the funds are in principle to be committed and spent in that same budget year.

Differentiated appropriations cover lines in the Budget where there are separate entries for 'commitment appropriations' and 'payment appropriations':

- ◆ *Commitment appropriations* cover the total cost, in the current financial year, of the legal obligations entered into for multiannual operations to be carried out over more than one financial year: for example, research or construction projects;
- ◆ The corresponding *payment appropriations* cover the expenditure in that year arising from the commitments then entered into, or carried over from preceding years.

Cancellations, carry-overs and transfers

The fact that funds have been committed, and corresponding payment appropriations made available, does not necessarily mean that the money will actually be spent. The Court of Auditors' report for 2009 shows that in certain areas the utilisation rate of payment appropriations in the Budget was well below 100%: for direct research (T10), for example, it was only 55.9%, with 42.7%

being carried over into 2010, and the rest cancelled. Overall, however, the utilisation rate of payments was 95% – a very much better figure than those which the Court castigated in the 1980s and 1990s.

The rules for dealing with unused appropriations are outlined in the Financial Regulation and the implementing regulations. In principle, appropriations which have not been used at the end of the financial year for which they were entered are cancelled, in accordance with the 'principle of annuality'. The unspent money contributed by Member States should then be credited back to them. It is, however, possible for such appropriations to be carried over to the next financial year, subject to certain conditions and limits. In the case of commitments, the rules implementing the Financial Regulation lay down the conditions for carry-over:

> "The commitment appropriations referred to in Article 9(2)
> (a) of the Financial Regulation may be carried over only if the
> commitments could not be made before 31 December of the
> financial year for reasons not attributable to the authorising
> officer and if the preparatory stages are sufficiently advanced
> to make it reasonable to surmise that the commitment will be
> made by no later than 31 March of the following year."

Payment appropriations may also be carried over to cover existing commitments or commitments linked to commitment appropriations carried over. Non-differentiated appropriations corresponding to obligations duly contracted at the close of the financial year are carried over automatically to the following financial year only.

In principle, too, appropriations entered into the Budget for a specific purpose and assigned to a specific item of expenditure can only be spent on that item – the 'principle of specification'. However, since the institutions require a certain flexibility of management, transfers between budgetary lines are possible, again subject to rules laid down in the Financial Regulation and implementing regulations. An institution may be allowed to carry out a transfer autonomously – in the case of the European Parliament, the responsibility lies with the Budgetary Control Committee; or it may first have to submit it to the budgetary authority (Council and Parliament) for information purposes or for a decision.

Chapter 5

Implementing the Budget

The Financial Regulation: the control of expenditure

The bulk of the Financial Regulation, and of the implementing regulations, deals with the implementation of the Budget following its adoption. Apart from the administrative expenditure of the various institutions, this is primarily the responsibility of the Commission. As the Regulation makes clear, however, implementation can in practice be carried out in a number of ways:

◆ Directly by the Commission's own departments, or by the Commission's executive agencies and other bodies set up by the EU;

◆ Indirectly by delegation to the Member States ('shared management') or to third countries ('decentralised management'), but with the Commission retaining ultimate responsibility;

◆ Jointly with international organisations ('joint management').

Many of the most serious past errors of budgetary management identified by the Court of Auditors and the Committee of Independent Experts concerned the internal Commission procedures for authorising, accounting for and internally auditing payments. These are the subject of detailed rules established in the Regulations, which define the separate responsibilities of authorising officers, accounting officers and internal auditors. The Regulations also lay down the basic principles governing public procurement, including advertising and information obligations; and the procedures for awarding, paying and controlling grants. Finally, there are rules on the presentation of accounts, and the procedures leading to the discharge, in particular the external audit by the Court of Auditors.

The Financial Regulation is subject to review at least every three years; and in May 2010 proposals for amendments – largely of a technical nature, but mostly involving simplification – were tabled by the Commission,[59] together with proposals for changes to the implementing regulations.[60] The Court of Auditors' opinion on the proposed changes was published in October that year,[61] and, while unsurprisingly calling for the rejection of proposed changes that would "constrain the ability of the Court to carry out its Treaty responsibilities effectively", concluded that "taken as a whole, the proposals contained in the recast of the Financial Regulation will provide opportunities for the Commission to improve transparency and financial management".

The problem of shared responsibility

As already noted, however, by far the largest proportion of the Budget falls under the 'shared management' category - a reality recognised in the Lisbon Treaty: the words "The Commission shall implement the budget" was replaced by "The Commission shall implement the budget in co-operation with the Member States".[62] It is in this context that the problems of control have proved most acute. The second 1999 report of the Committee of Experts outlined in some detail the problems raised by the fact that some 80% of the EU Budget is in practice administered by Member States, while the EU – that is, the Commission – remains accountable. "Where a fraud or irregularity goes undetected or unreported it is the Community budget, and not the Member State which pays".[63]

Member States, the report went on to observe, "have a conflict of interest":

---

59 COM(2010) 260 final of 28 May 2010.
60 SEC(2010) 639/2.
61 Opinion No 6/2010.
62 See new Treaty Chapter 4 'Implementation of the Budget and Discharge'.
63 op.cit. para 3.1.4.

"On the one hand, as members of the Council it is their duty in adopting regulations to create conditions for their implementation that are readily implemented and controlled by the Commission. On the other hand, as nation states they favour their own systems of management and control. This hybrid arrangement leads to a lack of clarity on mutual responsibilities and obligations and fails to give any guarantee that the right balance has been struck in the interests of good management of Community monies."[64]

In fact, the conflict of interest goes a great deal further. As already noted in the context of the *juste retour* controversy, national governments, anxious to receive as much as possible from the EU Budget, have had little incentive to investigate too diligently projects which qualify for EU funding. The Experts' report drily observed:

"it is difficult to believe that the administrative authorities or other bodies in the Member States are always inclined to highlight for the Commission instances of irregularity or negligence on their part which would result in them bearing the resulting financial consequences."[65]

The large number of instances where irregularity or fraud is actually revealed – notably in the case of the CAP – indicate the scale of the problem. Between 1989 and 1993, for example, some ECU 3.2bn had to be repaid by Italy and Spain after their failure to manage the milk quota scheme. In many countries CAP money has been disbursed, effectively unchecked, by hundreds of small *de facto* agencies.

It is also the case that certain broader policies have been an open invitation to fraud. One notorious example was the attempt during the 1970s and 1980s to maintain a single price structure

---

64 *op.cit.* para 3.5.3.
65 *op.cit.* para 3.7.5.

for agricultural products in the face of volatile exchange rates by creating a structure of artificial 'green' rates. As products crossed internal borders, discrepancies between the real rates and the green rates were evened out by charging, or paying out, Monetary Compensatory Amounts (MCAs). As a member of the European Parliament's Budgetary Control Committee, I was once given the task of reporting on the consequences of this system for the movement of agricultural products across the border between Northern Ireland and the Irish Republic. My findings were such as to have the report classified as 'internal only'; but it is not too difficult to guess what they were.[66]

A second example – one which survives intact today – can be found in the decision in 1992 to preserve the so-called 'destination' system for applying VAT to intra-Union movements of goods.[67] The details of the system are complex; but the net result is that products can move around the Single Market VAT-free; and much depends on accurate and honest record-keeping by traders. With the downgrading of the VAT element in the funding of the EU Budget, VAT fraud is now less of a problem for the EU itself; but, combined with fraud linked to the movement of excisable goods – particularly tobacco products and alcoholic beverages – has become a serious one for several Member States. Finance ministries regularly complain about the loss of revenue from 'carousel' and other VAT frauds; and in its Annual Report for 1998 the Court of Auditors observed:

---

[66] The BBC *Panorama* programme popularised this issue with tales of a pig which had been going backwards and forwards across the border collecting £7.50 in MCAs on each circuit.

[67] The alternative is the 'origin' system under which goods would move between, say, the UK and France in exactly the same way as they do between England and Scotland: i.e. with VAT already invoiced. This was the system proposed by the Single Market Commissioner in 1997, Lord Cockfield, but was rejected by national governments which feared loss of revenue as a result of the differences in national VAT rates and imbalances in trade flows.

"Following its work in respect of the regime governing VAT on intra-Community trade, the Court had noted a significant fall in VAT revenue in 1993. This fall could not be completely explained by technical or procedural factors. The question therefore was whether the new VAT regime for intra-Community trade was the direct cause of the fall in VAT revenue, in particular as the result of an increase in fraud and tax evasion."

The discharge

The importance in the evolution of the EU's budgetary procedures of the Court of Auditors' reports, and of the linked European Parliament votes on the discharge, has been described in Chapter 2. Arguably they have been of greater long-term significance than the budgetary procedure itself.

The discharge procedure is outlined in Treaty Articles 275 and 276. It begins formally when the Commission submits to the Council and the European Parliament the accounts and financial statements for the preceding financial year. The Council, acting by qualified majority, then makes a recommendation to the Parliament as to whether to grant the Commission a discharge as to the implementation of the Budget. The Parliament takes the final decision.

Before this can happen, however, both Council and Parliament will have taken account of the Court of Auditors' report for the year and of any relevant special report from the Court; and also of the Court's 'statement of assurance' as to the reliability of the accounts and the legality and regularity of the underlying transactions. The remit of the Court – laid down in Treaty Article 248 – is wide: it is required to "examine the accounts of all revenue and expenditure of the Community" and also examine "the accounts of all revenue and expenditure of all bodies set up by the Community". It has substantial investigative powers:

84

"The audit shall be based on records and, if necessary, performed on the spot in the other institutions of the Community, on the premises of any body which manages revenue or expenditure on behalf of the Community and in the Member States, including on the premises of any natural or legal person in receipt of payments from the budget. In the Member States the audit shall be carried out in liaison with national audit bodies or, if these do not have the necessary powers, with the competent national departments. The Court of Auditors and the national audit bodies of the Member States shall co-operate in a spirit of trust while maintaining their independence. These bodies or departments shall inform the Court of Auditors whether they intend to take part in the audit.

"The other institutions of the Community, any bodies managing revenue or expenditure on behalf of the Community, any natural or legal person in receipt of payments from the budget, and the national audit bodies or, if these do not have the necessary powers, the competent national departments, shall forward to the Court of Auditors, at its request, any document or information necessary to carry out its task."

The Commission is of course a participant in the procedure. Its replies to the Court's observations, together with the replies of the other EU institutions under examination, form part of the Court's Annual reports. The Commission may also be asked to give evidence directly to the Parliament – generally to its Budgetary Control Committee – and to submit additional information at the Parliament's request.

Refusing to grant the Commission a discharge has proved an important element in the evolution of the European Parliament's powers. Even when discharge *is* granted, however, this is not the end of the procedure. The Treaty then requires the Commission to "take all appropriate steps to act on the observations in the decisions giving discharge and on other observations by the European Parliament relating to the execution of expenditure, as well as on comments accompanying the recommendations on discharge adopted by the Council ..."

And, if asked by Parliament or Council, to

"report on the measures taken in the light of these observations and comments and in particular on the instructions given to the departments which are responsible for the implementation of the budget. These reports shall also be forwarded to the Court of Auditors."

Chapter 6
The 2011 Budget

Watering the wine

Though the new budgetary procedure established by the Lisbon Treaty was followed to the letter, the negotiations on the 2011 draft budget soon became entangled with an entirely different issue: the impending negotiations on the 2014–2020 multiannual financial framework (see next Chapter).

The Commission's original draft of the 2011 Budget had called for an increase in spending of 6.2% in payment appropriations over 2010, a position which was supported by the Parliament. The Council eventually agreed on a rise of 2.91% (though only a 0.22% rise in commitments, and with the Austrian, Czech, Danish, Finnish, Dutch, Swedish and the UK delegations voting against), and during the conciliation procedure Parliament offered to accept this – but at a price. This was an agreement on 'flexibility' within the Budget to deal with new priorities or upcoming urgencies; and on a seven-point 'political commitment' to be honoured by all sides in establishing the 2014–2020 Framework. This was in order, in the words of the Parliament's President Jerzy Buzek, "to avoid future budgetary crises". However, the Council – and in particular the representatives from the UK, Sweden and the Netherlands – initially rejected the offer; and in November 2010 it looked as though the following year would, once again, start with a Budget based on the system of twelfths.

This would have been extremely embarrassing for at least one important reason: it would have made it impossible – or at least extremely difficult – to fund the new External Action Service: the EU's 'diplomatic corps' set up under the Lisbon Treaty. Expenditure under the system of twelfths can only be made on the basis of lines established under the previous year's Budget; and no provision at all was made in the 2010 Budget for funding the Action Service.

No doubt it was with such potential embarrassments in mind that, by the time the Parliament came to its final vote on the

Budget at the December 2010 part-session, a compromise had been found.

As far as payment appropriations were concerned, the Council's 'austerity' proposals were accepted. Parliament, for its part, was able to insert extra commitment appropriations for projects such as the Lifelong Learning Programme (+€18m), the Entrepreneurship and Innovation Programme (+€10m), the Intelligent Energy – Europe Programme (+€10m), the Baltic Sea strategy (+€2.5m), the management of fishery resources (+€2m) and an extra amount of +€100m for Palestine, the peace process and UNRWA (the United Nations Relief and Works Agency). There was also a joint statement outlining Parliament's role in framing the 2014–2020 Framework and in discussions on new 'own resources', the possibility of which was opened up by the Lisbon Treaty (see the final section of Chapter 1).

"Everyone", the President-in-Office of the Council, Wathelet Melchior, told Parliament during the December 2010 budget debate in Strasbourg, "had to put water in the wine".

One or two issues nevertheless still remained unresolved at the end of 2010, in particular that of the so-called flexibility instrument of 0.03% of GNI per annum, or roughly €4bn, to cover unexpected needs. In the past, activation of this instrument had been decided by a qualified majority in Council; but during the negotiations on the 2011 Budget, a number of countries, including the UK, insisted that in future unanimity should be required.

The figures

Section Three of the 2011 Budget starts with figures for the EU Commission's own revenues, which are estimated to come to some €1.2bn. This is income entirely separate from the funding coming from, or *via*, the Member States, and so can be considered genuine own resources. The largest item, some €890m, is "revenue accruing from persons working with the institutions and other

Union bodies" – i.e. taxes and pension contributions paid by EU officials. The second largest is "interest on late payment and fines", mostly paid by companies found to be in breach of competition policy, but also "penalty payments and lump sums imposed on a Member State for not complying with a judgment of the Court of Justice of the European Union on its failure to fulfil an obligation under the Treaty". The figure optimistically entered here for 2011 is a 'p.m.' (*pour mémoire* – i.e. a token entry); but the Budget shows that Member States were obliged to pay out nearly €17m in such fines in 2009.

As far as expenditure is concerned, in terms of the current financial framework, the figures eventually voted were as in Table 6.1.

Table 6.1: The Commission budget for 2011

	Comparison 2010 Budget* (€m)		Financial framework 2011 (€m)		Final Budget 2011 (€m)	
	Commit.	Payments	Commit.	Payments	Commit.	Payments
1a. Competitiveness for growth and employment	14,863	11,343	12,987	-	13,521	11,628
1b. Cohesion for growth and employment	49,387	36,371	50,987	-	50,981	41,652
2. Preservation and management of natural resources	59,499	58,136	60,338	-	58,659	56,379
3a. Freedom security and justice	1,006	739	1,206	-	1,139	813
3b. Citizenship	681	672	683	-	683	646
4. The EU as a global partner	8,141	7,788	8,430	-	8,754	7,238
5. Administration	7,907	7,907	8,334	-	8,173	8,172
Total	141,484	122,955	142,965	134,280	141,909	126,527
As % of GNI	1.17%	1.02 %	1.14 %	1.07 %	1.13%	1.01 %

Note: * Including amending Budgets 1–7

Source: European Parliament

The financial framework nomenclature, although important from the point of view of financial control and the identification of priorities, is nevertheless not much use as a way of identifying particular items of expenditure. For this, the breakdown of the Budget into 32 Titles, each further broken down into Chapters, is more helpful, and also gives a better idea of the policies which the Budget finances. The Titles are shown in Table 6.2.

Table 6.2: Budget Titles

1: Economic and financial affairs	2: Enterprise
3: Competition	4: Employment and social affairs
5: Agriculture and rural development	6: Mobility and transport
7: Environment and climate action	8: Research
9: Information society and media	10: Direct research
11: Maritime affairs and fisheries	12: Internal market
13: Regional policy	14: Taxation and customs union
15: Education and culture	16: Communication
17: Health and consumer protection	18: Freedom, security and justice
19: External relations	20: Trade
21: Development and relations with african, Caribbean and pacific (acp) states	22: Enlargement
23: Humanitarian aid	24: Fight against fraud
25: Commission's policy co-ordination and legal advice	26: Commission's administration
27: Budget	28: Audit
29: Statistics	30: Pensions & related expenditure
31: Language services	32: Energy

There is also a 33rd Title, Reserves, which is numbered 40 to allow for the addition of new operational Titles.

The detailed budget for each of these Titles distinguishes between the planned operational expenditure, and the Commission's estimated staff and administrative costs in carrying it out.

The other Sections of the Budget, covering the almost exclusively administrative costs of the EU's other institutions, are naturally only a very small proportion of the EU total, and in the

Understanding the EU Budget

past a convention has been established under which the two parts of the budgetary authority, i.e. Parliament and Council, do not interfere with each other's budgets (nor with those of the other institutions, apart, of course, from the Commission). In recent years, nevertheless, these subsidiary budgets have begun to attract some critical attention – particularly that of the European Parliament. The 2011 figures are shown in Table 6.3.

Table 6.3: The 2011 budgets of the other institutions (€m)

European Parliament	1,685.8
Council and European Council	563.3
European Court of Justice	341.2
Court of Auditors	118.8
Economic and Social Committee	90.2
Committee of the Regions	62.1
European Ombudsman	9.4
European Data Protection Supervisor	2.0
European External Action Service	464.1

Source: EU Budget

Chapter 7
The future

Searching finance

The 2014–2020 financial framework

As became clear during the 2011 Budget procedure, the preliminary skirmishes in establishing the multiannual financial framework (MFF) for the Budgets between 2014 and 2020 were already well under way in the closing months of 2010. The Commission has been required to present its proposals before 1 July 2011; after which it will need to be adopted, by majority in the European Parliament, but by unanimity in Council – i.e. every Member State, including the UK, will have a veto.

Establishing the framework will involve three key decisions:

◆ How large should the Budgets be?
◆ What should be the budgetary priorities? and
◆ How should the Budgets be financed?

The first of these issues has, not surprisingly, already become the subject of heated debate, not least between Member State governments. In an open letter to the Commission published in December 2010, the UK, France, Germany, Finland and The Netherlands argued forcefully that EU expenditure should be frozen, in real terms, for the duration of the framework. Payments in any one year, in this case, could not exceed the current 1% of EU GDP. Some have gone further, arguing that, as public expenditure in many Member States is due to fall in real terms over the next few years, the same should be true of the EU.

The counter argument is that, since the Lisbon Treaty has given the EU substantial new tasks, particularly in the field of foreign policy, commensurate budgetary increases are inevitable. The countries of Central and Eastern Europe that joined the EU in 2004 and 2007, whose per capita incomes are still well below the EU average, have – as they see it – legitimate expectations of budgetary transfers through the Cohesion and other funds. Finally, there are growing calls for major expenditure in such fields as R&D and the improvement of infrastructures in order to improve the international competitivity of Member States' economies and that of the EU as a whole. An indication of what is at issue was the Commission's opening bid for the 2012 Budget: an increase of 4.9% in payment appropriations – needed, it argued, to fund commitments already entered into. Not surprisingly, the UK Chancellor of the Exchequer, George Osborne, described the proposal as "completely unacceptable".

Meeting existing obligations and expectations is, of course, not incompatible with budgetary restraint; but would involve a major adjustment of budgetary priorities.

Expenditure was classified under the same eight broad headings in the first three financial perspectives: Delors I (1988–92), Delors II (1993–99) and Agenda 2000 (2000–06). The headings of the 2007–2013 Framework (see Table 4.2) were somewhat different, but basically covered the same fields. Table 6.3 shows the average annual figures on a comparable basis.

Despite the slight decline in agricultural spending over the years, and the increases in spending on regional aid and cohesion, it is clear that the priorities have not changed greatly. As the economist Daniel Gros at the Centre for European Policy Studies has argued, they are above all a legacy of the past:

> "The current composition of spending is the result of historical accidents. The key driving force behind the two items that now dominate the budget – agriculture and regional aid – was the perception in a darker past that Europe needed to ensure its own food supply and, in the 1980s and 1990s, that poorer member countries needed to be bribed to accept the internal market and monetary union. The main legacy of the 'founding' compromises on agriculture and Structural Funds is that the budget is basically seen as a vehicle for the

Understanding the EU Budget

redistribution of money between member states, rather than a tool for fostering common goals."[68]

Table 7.1: Financial frameworks 1998–2013

	Delors I (1988–92) ECU m)	Delors II (1993–99) ECU m	Agenda 2000 (2000–06) ECU m	2007–2013 €m
Agriculture	28 440	36 503	42 534	57 808*
Structural Operations	10 628	25 200	30 430	49 273
Internal Policies	1 862	4 512	6 261	21 609**
External Actions	2 498	5 200	8 100	13 656
Administration	4 540	3 640	4 809	4 089
Reserves, etc.	1 000	643	179	

Note: Annual average appropriations for commitment
* Including €14,797m for rural development.
** Including €2,644m for "Citizenship, freedom, security and justice".

Source: European Commission

It is indeed true that the 2007–2013 budgetary priorities have been noticeably out of line with the wider priorities for the EU as established in 2000 under the so-called Lisbon Strategy.[69] The objective then adopted by the European Council was to make the EU "the most competitive and dynamic knowledge-based economy in the world...", and targets were set for employment, research, innovation, information and communication technologies and education, economic reform and 'social cohesion'. The Strategy was updated in 2001, and again in 2005; but despite efforts by the Commission to focus more funds on the Lisbon targets, and despite its assertion that "the EU budget has

---

68 Daniel Gros: *How to Achieve a Better Budget for the European Union* (Centre for European Policy Studies, 2008)
69 See Presidency Conclusions to the Lisbon European Council, 23 and 24 March 2000.

proved itself as an effective tool to realise the EU's aspirations and implement its policies",[70] the Budgets between 2007 and 2011 can hardly be said to have brought the EU much closer to being the most dynamic economy in the world.

In succession to the Lisbon Strategy, the Commission in 2010 proposed a 'Europe 2020' Strategy,[71] with five key objectives:

◆ 75% of 20–64 year-olds to be employed;

◆ 3% of the EU's GDP (public and private combined) to be invested in R&D/innovation;

◆ Greenhouse gas emissions 20% (or even 30%, if a satisfactory international agreement can be achieved to follow Kyoto) lower than 1990; 20% of energy from renewables; and a 20% increase in energy efficiency;

◆ Reducing school drop-out rates below 10% and at least 40% of 30–34-year-olds completing third level education (or equivalent); and

◆ At least 20m fewer people in or at risk of poverty and social exclusion.

Taken together, the Commission estimates that when these targets are achieved, the result could be an extra 4% on EU GDP and 5.6m new jobs by 2020.[72]

---

70 In the 2010 *Budget Review*.

71 *Europe 2020: A European strategy for smart, sustainable and inclusive growth* (European Commission, COM(2010)2020, 3 March 2010).

72 See *Quantifying the potential macroeconomic effects of the Europe 2020 strategy: stylised scenarios* (European Commission Economic Papers n°424. September 2010) and *Macroeconomic effects of Europe 2020: stylised scenarios* (ECFIN Economic Briefs 2010 n°11).

The Budget Review

Given its overall objective, the most critical elements of the Lisbon Strategy were the targets for research and innovation; and the same is likely to be true of Europe 2020, given the growing threats to the competitivity of Europe in the world economy. These threats, of course, are not something new: there were fears in the 1960s and 1970s (as expressed, for example, in a best-seller of 1967, *Le Défi Americain*,[73]) that Europe would never be able to compete with the United States as long as the US federal budget, and the defence budget in particular, could ensure US technological superiority.

The Commission envisages the EU Budget playing a major part in meeting the Europe 2020 objective: "at the core of the 2020 strategy", the Budget Review declares, "is the need to support the transformation of the European economy towards an economy based on knowledge and innovation." If this is to happen, however, there will have to be either a substantial increase in the size of the Budget, or a substantial shift away from spending on agriculture and financial transfers, and towards investment. Between 2007 and 2013 the proportion of the EU Budget devoted to R&D expenditure will have doubled – but only to 7% of the total. An alliance of 22 prominent European research-intensive universities, including the universities of Oxford and Cambridge – the League of European Research Universities (LERU) – has recently called for a doubling again in the 2014–20 financial perspective. But even 14% of a frozen budget will be relatively small beer.

The counter-argument to a massive increase in EU spending on R&D, of course, is that centralised public spending does not, at least in the UK, have a particularly good track record for creating global winners or stimulating innovation; and there must be strong doubts as to whether the EU Commission would do much

---

73 *Le Défi Americain* by Jean-Jacques Servan-Schreiber (Denoël, 1967).

better. More fruitful, perhaps, than huge EU-funded projects are subsidies of the 'pump-priming' kind – exactly the kind of projects, in fact, that the EU Budget already finances, and which the Commission envisages playing an important role in the 2014–2020 period. As the Budget Review puts it:

> "With the European Research Council and the European Institute for Technology, the EU has put in place a fresh new approach to promoting excellence on a European scale and forging the links between education, research and business so critical to seeing creativity carry through into growth."

In any case, the most successful large-scale EU-level projects so far – for example the Space Launcher – have been funded inter-governmentally rather than through the EU Budget. Very substantial investments are also made though the European Investment Bank (EIB), which operates successfully on a commercial basis, subject to broad political guidelines; and also the European Bank for Reconstruction and Development (EBRD).

In the field of infrastructure, the Commission envisages quite ambitious action:

> "a European core transport network shifting freight and passenger flows towards more sustainable transport modes; high-speed broadband available in every part of the EU; and an energy network capable of delivering on the promise of the internal market, accessing new energy sources and exploiting new smart technologies."

Expenditure from the EU Budget would need to be combined with finance from other sources: the EIB, the EBRD, national budgets and private investment. The Budget Review indeed envisages the creation of "innovative financial instruments": for example, 'EU project bonds'. Appropriations from the EU Budget would enhance the credit rating of chosen projects, enabling them to attract commercial finance.

Budgetary goals identified by the Commission include "kick-starting investment in the greener technologies and greener services" and the "the greening of direct aids" within the CAP; a focus of resources on the poorest regions and Member States; a "comprehensive European Employment initiative" to improve "skills, mobility, adaptability and participation"; "promoting fundamental rights and EU values"; and "effective border management". Overarching these individual goals was the need for "greater concentration and coherence": targeting resources on priority areas, and co-ordinating the expenditures made within different programmes.

The Commission also stresses the importance of expenditure relating to the EU's external role in the world. For example, it was "particularly important to improve the Union's ability to respond to large-scale conflicts or disasters". Combating global poverty was "one of the EU's core goals", and Member States were committed, collectively, to dedicating 0.7% of GNI by 2015 to official development aid. Channelling aid through the EU, the Commission goes on to argue, provides a good example of 'added value': it offered "a global reach" compared to Member States' concentration on a limited number of partners. Financing the EU's 'neighbourhood' policies was also important "to secure long-term prosperity and stability...close to its borders" – an objective which has become unexpectedly topical as a result of the popular, 'Arab Spring' uprisings in North Africa and the Middle East.

Finally, in the case of administrative expenditure, "a rigorous search for increased efficiency and performance in administrative resources" was required.

It is difficult to disagree with much of this Commission wish-list. Whether all the goals are attainable within the framework of 'frozen' Budgets is another matter. The UK Government's initial reactions were given in written evidence to the House of Lords Select Committee on the European Union in January 2011 by the Economic Secretary to the Treasury, Justine Greening MP. There was support for the key objective of EU budgetary support for R&D and innovation, "but not at the cost of a larger overall budget".

Greening also placed especial emphasis on the need for genuine added value: "beneficial outcomes achieved through EU-level action that are additional to those achievable by Member States' acting alone". Adequate evidence of EU added value was often lacking, and the Government wanted "to encourage a more outcomes-focused policy development in the EU". Moreover, "it did not follow that all spending proposals that demonstrably deliver EU added value should be funded. Instead, other important tests apply, including subsidiarity."

> "In difficult economic times, public expenditure programmes need to deliver greater value-added than before. At the margin, this means that the poorest performing programmes should be revised or discontinued."

There was a cautious welcome for the Commission's proposals for new financing instruments, such as EU project bonds, designed to "leverage and stimulate private investment". The role of the EU Budget in the fields of energy and climate change received strong support: "climate change cannot be effectively tackled by individual nations acting alone." And traditional UK support for lower spending on the CAP was reaffirmed: the Government wanted to see agriculture "becoming competitive without reliance on subsidies".

The view of the Parliament

In June 2010, in order to prepare for negotiations on the new MFF, the European Parliament established a committee – the Special Policy Challenges Committee (SURE) – on "the policy challenges and budgetary resources for a sustainable European Union

Understanding the EU Budget

after 2013". The Committee's report was adopted on 26 May[74] and incorporated the opinions of eight other parliamentary committees, including those dealing with regional development and agriculture.[75]

Though much of the report covered ground on which there was already broad agreement between the Commission and Member State Governments – the 2020 strategy as the policy reference for the financial framework; the need for demonstrable European added value (EAV); a shift towards investment; improved co-ordination between the European and the national budgets; maximising the impact of EU funding by leveraging public and private financial resources; innovative financing; and tight controls over spending – there were also signs of lively arguments to come. On the key issue of the Budgets' size the report was

> "of the firm opinion that freezing the EU budget, as demanded by some Member States, should not be considered a viable option as it would be detrimental for the achievement of the Union's agreed objectives and could lead to less efficient individual Member States' spending".

Instead, the report called for increases of at least 5% over the 2013 level. Even this, it observed, would go only a small way towards financing the actions to which not just the Parliament, but the Member States as well, were already committed. The MEPs challenged the countries calling for a budgetary freeze to say which of these actions – for example, the planned boost for research and

---

74 *Investing in the future: a new Multiannual Financial Framework (MFF) for a competitive, sustainable and inclusive Europe. Rapporteur:* Salvador Garriga Polledo (PE458.649. A7-0193/2011).

75 The report also noted that it had received input from the Austrian *Nationalrat*, the Czech Chamber, the Danish *Folkentinget*, the Estonian *Riigikogu*, the *Deutscher Bundestag*, the *Deutscher Bundesrat*, the Irish *Oireachtas*, the Lithuanian *Seimas*, the Latvian *Saeima*, the Portuguese *Assembleia da República*, the Dutch *Tweede Kamer*, and the Swedish *Riksdagen*.

innovation, investment in infrastructure, foreign policy priorities, including enlargement, and the funding of the European Financial Stability Mechanism – they now wished to drop.

The report also addressed one of the main problems inherent in a multiannual programme: the need for the right balance between "stability, medium-term predictability and flexibility". The report accepted the seven-year timescale as a transitional solution, but insisted that a Mid-term Review "should become a legally binding obligation enshrined in the MFF regulation". There should then be a 'five plus five' structure: a 10-year framework, revised halfway through, which would be aligned with the European Parliament's five-year mandates. Such a structure had earlier been supported by Commission President Barroso.

The report also addressed the issue of unused margins, de-committed and unused appropriations (both commitments and payments) in annual budgets. These

> "should be carried over to the next year and constitute a global MFF margin to be attributed to the different headings according to their estimated needs … and not returned to the Member States, as is currently the case".

There should, in any case, be a substantial global margin to increase flexibility; and appropriations for large strategic investments such as the Galileo satellite project should be ring-fenced.

The whole Parliament voted through on the report on 9 June, in advance of the Commission's own proposals, published at the end of the same month.

The Commission proposals

The Commission published its own proposals for the 2014–20 MFF at the end of June 2011.[76] In rough, overall terms, it split the difference between the Parliament's +5% as a share of Member States' national income and the Council's standstill. Over the seven years it proposed commitments amounting to just over €1,000bn (in 2011 prices), and payments of slightly less, overall still equal to only 1% of projected GNI (not counting various emergency and other funds outside the MFF amounting to another €58bn), as shown in Table 7.2.

"This is an innovative Budget", Commission President Barroso declared in his foreword to the document. The proposals in fact follow closely the priorities outlined in the earlier Budget Review and the linkage with the Europe 2020 strategy. To strengthen the link, the Commission proposes a new principle of 'conditionality' – Member States and those receiving EU money "will be required to demonstrate that the funding received is being used to further the achievement of EU policy priorities".

These priorities include measure to close the EU's 'innovation gap': €80bn for the 'Common Strategic Framework for Research and Innovation'. They also include a €40bn 'Connecting Europe Facility' to "accelerate the infrastructure development that the EU needs". Spending on Home Affairs (€8.2bn) would be consolidated into a Migration and Asylum Fund and an Internal Security Fund.

The bulk of the proposed spending, however, continues to be concentrated on 'cohesion policy instruments' (€376bn, with a more refined classification of eligible regions); and the CAP: €281.8bn for agriculture, plus €89.9bn for 'rural development'

---

76 *A Budget for Europe 2020: Communication from the Commission to the European Parliament, the Council, the European Economic and Social Committee and the Committee of the Regions* (COM(2011) 500 final, 29.6.2011).

and €15.2bn for other purposes such as food safety – justified, in Barroso's words, because "EU funding is less expensive than 27 national agricultural policies".

The Commission admits that there are still defects in implementation procedures and control requirements. "Changes over the years have given rise to a system that is now widely regarded as too complicated and often discouraging participation and/or delaying implementation." Accordingly, there will be "radical simplification across the whole future MFF". The number of separate programmes will be reduced, and the administration of EU institutions, agencies and other bodies will be simplified and rationalised, leading to a 5% reduction in staffing levels.

The MFF would be structured under five broad headings:

1. Smart and Inclusive Growth.
2. Sustainable Growth: Natural Resources.
3. Security and citizenship.
4. Global Europe.
5. Administration.

The most contentious of the Commission's proposals, however, will almost certainly be those relating to the way in which future Budgets are to be financed, linked to the perennial issue of countries' net budgetary balances. The time has come, the Commission paper observes, "to move away from the 'my money back' attitude …".

Table 7.2: The 2014–2020 MFF: The Commission proposals (€m)

(EUR million - 2011 prices)

COMMITMENT APPROPRIATIONS	2014	2015	2016	2017	2018	2019	2020	Total 2014-2020
1. Smart and Inclusive Growth	**64 696**	**66 580**	**68 133**	**69 956**	**71 596**	**73 768**	**76 179**	**490 908**
of which: Economic, social and territorial cohesion	50 468	51 543	52 542	53 609	54 798	55 955	57 105	376 020
2. Sustainable Growth: Natural Resources	**57 386**	**56 527**	**55 702**	**54 861**	**53 837**	**52 829**	**51 784**	**382 927**
of which: Market related expenditure and direct payments	42 244	41 623	41 029	40 420	39 618	38 831	38 060	281 825
3. Security and citizenship	**2 532**	**2 571**	**2 609**	**2 648**	**2 687**	**2 726**	**2 763**	**18 535**
4. Global Europe	**9 400**	**9 645**	**9 845**	**9 960**	**10 150**	**10 380**	**10 620**	**70 000**
5. Administration	**8 542**	**8 679**	**8 796**	**8 943**	**9 073**	**9 225**	**9 371**	**62 629**
of which: Administrative expenditure of the institutions	6 967	7 039	7 108	7 191	7 288	7 385	7 485	50 464
TOTAL COMMITMENT APPROPRIATIONS	**142 556**	**144 002**	**145 085**	**146 368**	**147 344**	**148 928**	**150 718**	**1 025 000**
as a percentage of GNI	1.08%	1.07%	1.06%	1.06%	1.05%	1.04%	1.03%	1.05%
TOTAL PAYMENT APPROPRIATIONS	**133 851**	**141 278**	**135 516**	**138 396**	**142 247**	**142 916**	**137 994**	**972 198**
as a percentage of GNI	1.01%	1.05%	0.99%	1.00%	1.01%	1.00%	0.94%	1.00%
OUTSIDE THE MFF								
Emergency Aid Reserve	350	350	350	350	350	350	350	2 450
European Globalisation Fund	429	429	429	429	429	429	429	3 000
Solidarity Fund	1 000	1 000	1 000	1 000	1 000	1 000	1 000	7 000
Flexibility instrument	500	500	500	500	500	500	500	3 500
Reserve for crises in the agricultural sector	500	500	500	500	500	500	500	3 500
ITER	886	624	299	291	261	232	114	2 707
GMES	834	834	834	834	834	834	834	5 841
EDF ACP	3 271	4 300	4 348	4 407	4 475	4 554	4 644	29 998
EDF OCT	46	46	46	46	46	46	46	321
Global Climate and Biodiversity Fund	p.m.	p.m.	p.m.	p.m.	p.m.	p.m.	p.m.	p.m.
TOTAL OUTSIDE THE MFF	**7 815**	**8 583**	**8 306**	**8 357**	**8 395**	**8 445**	**8 416**	**58 316**
TOTAL MFF + OUTSIDE MFF	**150 371**	**152 585**	**153 391**	**154 725**	**155 739**	**157 372**	**159 134**	**1 083 316**
as a percentage of GNI	1.13%	1.13%	1.12%	1.12%	1.11%	1.10%	1.09%	1.11%

Source: European Commission

Accordingly, and following an "extensive analysis of the options"[77], it proposes a new own resources system. The existing, purely statistical VAT element would be scrapped and the direct payments from national budgets reduced. Instead there would be two new EU taxes:

- ◆ A financial transactions tax (FTT): for example, a 0.1% tax on sales/purchases of bonds and shares;[78]
- ◆ A new VAT resource: an EU VAT of, say, 1% levied on transactions subject to the standard VAT rate.

These were preferred to the 'green' options of a tax on aviation, energy use, or revenue from the EU's Emission Trading System; and also to an EU Corporate Income Tax.

Rebates

The changes would also be linked to "an important simplification to the problem of rebates and corrections". The basic 'Fontainebleau' principle is to limit the net contributions of countries otherwise facing "a budgetary burden which is excessive in relation to their relative prosperity." At present, however, there is imperfect correlation between the relative prosperity of net contributing countries and their budgetary balances, as shown in Figure 7.1.

---

77 *See Financing the EU Budget: report on the operation of the own resources system* (Commission Staff Working Paper SEC(2011) 876 final of 29.6.2 011).

78 This could be a pragmatic first step towards the development of a FTT at world level (a Tobin Tax).

Figure 7.1: Prosperity and net payments into the EU Budget, average 2007–10

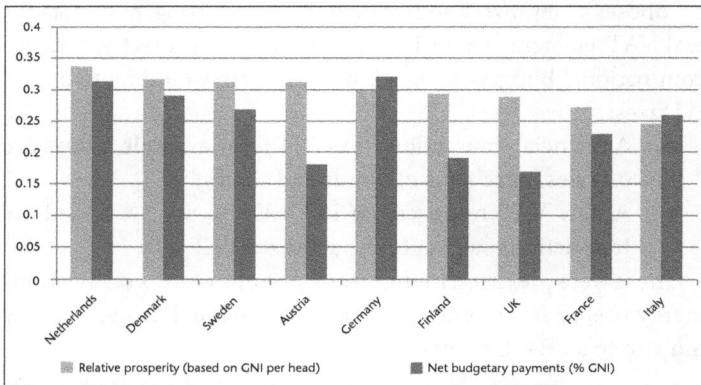

Source: European Commission, DG Budget

Moreover, the "correction maze", the complex system of annual rebates and "rebates on rebates", the Commission observes, has resulted in a most Member States perceiving "their contributions to or benefits from the EU budget as being unfair". Instead, there should be a single lump sum payment to eligible countries. That to the UK would amount to about €25bn for the 2014–20 period, as compared to annual payments which have fluctuated between nearly €7bn (2007) and just over €3.5bn (2009) in recent years.

Although, in principle, the UK rebate should amount to 66% of the difference between what it pays to the EU Budget (except the 'traditional own resources') and what it receives, calculating its size – and how paying for it is shared out between other Member States – is a far from straightforward operation (for details see SEC(2011)876). It has also had the perverse effect that money received by the UK to fund worthwhile projects is wholly or in part cancelled out by reductions in the rebate.

Future financing

In proposing these reforms, the Commission argues that its is not "about giving the EU fiscal sovereignty", but rather "returning...to the original intention of the treaties". As outlined earlier, this intention was that – as in the case of the ECSC – expenditure would be fully covered by own resources: that is, revenue that came directly to the EC/EU without being part of national taxation.

It can be argued that this is true of the so-called 'traditional own resources' consisting of customs duties and sugar levies paid by sugar producers. But these now only cover about 14% of spending. At one time it was thought that virtually the entire balance would be made up by the own resource based on Value Added Tax. Again as outlined earlier, it soon became clear that, as an indicator of relative economic strength, VAT was seriously defective. Moreover, calling the VAT element an own resource was always disingenuous, since in practice the payments into the Budget came out of general national taxation; and today the VAT element funds only 11% of expenditure. As a result, the bulk of EU spending is now funded by the 'balancing item' based on Member States' GNI, and paid directly by national exchequers out of general national taxation. The result is "a confusing and opaque mix of contributions from national budgets, corrections and rebates".[79]

This situation, indeed, has several drawbacks, one of which has already been discussed: the Council's and the European Parliament's asymmetry of perception. For the national governments in the Council, funding the EU Budget is just another element of national public expenditure, and subject to the same constraints. But the European Parliament is concerned only with expenditure – it doesn't need to worry about voting the necessary (and almost certainly unpopular) taxation.

---

[79] From the 2010 *Budget Review*.

Understanding the EU Budget

The case for genuine 'EU taxation' is not, therefore, solely based on the ambitions of federalists. Obliging the European Parliament to vote through the rates of a separate EU VAT – or of the other taxes currently under discussion – might markedly improve budgetary discipline. In addition, as Gros has argued,

> "Another beneficial change, which does not require a change in the Treaty, would be to synchronise the MYFP [multi-year financial perspectives] reference period with Parliament office terms, so as to strengthen the interrelation between budgetary decisions and European election results. The MYFP should run for five years, and enter into force one year after a new Parliament's election, to allow it sufficient time to deliberate after an election. With this change, MYFP content would become a main theme in Parliament election campaigns, with a likely increase in voter interest in the elections and their results."[80]

All proposals for new sources of EU revenue are nevertheless bound to face stiff opposition, not least from the UK Government. As Justine Greening observed in her evidence to the House of Lords, "the Government has been clear that we will not support any effort to introduce a new EU tax." Greening, indeed, went further. Taxation was "an issue of national sovereignty" and, in consequence, the Government was against *any* direct funding of the EU Budget. Although this was not spelt out, the statement was in effect a rejection of the own resources concept itself, despite its justification in the Treaty.

This view was in flat contradiction with that in the European Parliament's report, which argued:

> "the way the EU system of own resources has evolved, gradually being replaced by national contributions and consequently being perceived as an excessive burden on

---

[80] *op.cit.*

national public finances, renders its reform more necessary than ever. It places disproportionate emphasis on net cash flows to and from Member States, thus diluting the European common interest."

In addition, it agreed with the Commission that "the existing exceptions and correction mechanisms should be progressively phased out" – including, of course, the UK rebate.

Fiscal federalism

Creating a genuine federal level of taxation in the EU would also have important economic consequences. At a total level amounting to around 1% of GDP these would not be too serious – national parliaments setting levels of central taxation already have to take account of taxation levied at devolved levels: state, regional and local. But if the EU Budget were to expand to the kind of levels envisaged by, for example, the 1977 MacDougall report referred to in Chapter 1, an entirely new dimension would be added to the conduct of fiscal policy.

'Fiscal federalism' has been the subject of numerous studies by economists. One, published in 2005 – i.e. at the time the current Fiscal Framework was under discussion – was by Professor Iain Begg at the London School of Economics' European Institute. "From a public finance perspective", he argued, "the EU is a quasi-federal system[81] that lends itself to analysis using the tools of fiscal federalism."

Theories of fiscal federalism are, essentially, about 'who does and pays for what' at different levels of government in order to

---

[81] Iain Begg, *op.cit*. "The terms 'union', 'federation', 'supranational' and 'federal' – all of which are employed in the relevant academic literature – will, for the most part, be used interchangeably to refer to the highest tier of government or governance. Although the sensitivities of the 'f-word' in the UK context are well-known, from an analytic perspective the precise formulation makes no real difference".

maximise economic efficiency and welfare. As with all such economic questions there are trade-offs. If services are organised at lower tiers of jurisdiction, for example, there is always a 'freeloader' danger: non-residents may enjoy the benefits without paying the taxes to finance them, with the result that the levels of investment in the services in question are distorted. Transferring to a higher tier might avoid such spillover effects, produce economies of scale and ensure an optimum level of provision, but risks making the services remote from citizens and weakening democratic control.

There are other trade-offs. Providing services and raising taxes at devolved levels creates scope for competition between jurisdictions, encouraging efficiency and value for money. The same competition can, however, also lead to a 'race to the bottom', both in the standards of the services themselves and the tax base needed to fund them. It is also generally accepted that tax systems and public services should include some redistributive elements, both between sections of the population and geographical regions, which need to be organised centrally. In the UK, for example, the apparent post-code lottery in the provision of some medical services arouses considerable public resentment.

In addition, there are trade-offs of a non-economic kind. Begg quotes the distinguished former IMF economist Vito Tanzi,[82] who has observed that, despite being closer to the citizen, decentralised tiers of government tend to be more open to corruption "either because the calibre of officials is lower or because institutions are less developed..." In addition, "each time one adds another layer of government...the number of damaging regulations is likely to increase" – a view which will ring a bell with those who dislike 'Brussels'.

---

[82] V. Tanzi, *On fiscal federalism: issues to worry about* (IMF, 2000).

At whatever level services are provided, taxes must be levied to fund them; and economic theory suggests that the appropriate revenues should be raised, as far as possible, at the same level of government as that at which the services are delivered. This is the rationale behind the provisions in the Treaties for EU budgetary expenditure to be funded by own resources. Different forms of taxation, however, are more or less efficient at different levels of government. Where the tax base is mobile, as in the case of corporate taxes on multi-national companies, tax avoidance and 'jurisdiction shopping' can be prevented by levying the tax at the highest possible level. This, as outlined in Chapter 1, is the principal argument for an EU-level corporate tax. An alternative, which certain Member States are attempting to pursue, and others are resisting fiercely, is the harmonisation of national corporate taxation.

There are also arguments for levying certain elements of personal income tax at higher levels. This can be the case where there two or more separate jurisdictions have a claim to the same revenue streams: the country or countries in which the income in generated, and the country or countries in which the taxpayers have residence. Such problems are currently handled by a network of bilateral tax agreements; but not entirely satisfactorily, as the debates leading to the EU Directive on the taxation of interest on savings[83] – or the issue of 'non-doms' in the UK – made clear.

---

[83] At least three attempts were made by the Commission to introduce a Directive on the taxation of savings. The last was published in 1998 (*Draft Directive to ensure a minimum of effective taxation of savings income in the form of interest payments within the Community,* COM(1998)295), and was eventually adopted as Directive 2003/48/EC (see *Official Journal* L157/38 of 26.6.2003). For most EU Member States, the Directive provided for the exchange of information between national tax authorities. In the case of others like Luxembourg, however, the country where the interest is paid levies a withholding tax, a proportion of which is remitted to the country where the receiver of the interest is resident - but without the taxpayer being identified.

By contrast, where the tax base is immobile – as is the case, for example, with real estate – taxation can be levied at very decentralised levels. In between are taxes such as sales taxes, excise duties and VAT, which can be levied at decentralised levels, provided that there is not too great a disparity in rates. This is, in fact, the situation within the EU as a result of the Directives on indirect taxation adopted in the early 1990s as part of the Single Market programme (though the incidence of fraud indicates that the spread of rates, particularly in the case of excise duties, may still be too great).

Finally, there is the role of fiscal policy in economic stabilisation. In orthodox theory this is best carried out at the highest level, or at least at the same level as monetary policy. As noted in Chapter 1, however, the EU Budget is far too small to have any such stabilising role. Instead, in so far as any stabilising fiscal policies are pursued at EU level, this has to be through the horizontal co-ordination of the separate national budgetary policies – though recent experience suggests that achieving this will be very much more difficult than was believed at the time of the Maastricht Treaty negotiations.

Relevance to the EU Budget

It has to be asked, therefore: how relevant are theories of fiscal federalism to the actual situation in the EU, and in particular to the EU Budget? "Fiscal federalism", Begg comments, "is predicated on the jurisdictions all belonging to a single nation", which is very far from the case with the EU, despite those who hope for – or fear – a European super-state. In the case of the EU Budget, a "curious hybrid", it was "far from obvious that principles of public finance…had much influence on developments". And, more generally, the principle of subsidiarity, now enshrined in the Treaty,[84] was "inimical to the development of a system that accords better with fiscal federalism". In sum, what should be pursued from the point of view of economic efficiency and the maximisation of overall welfare, appears politically impossible.

The extreme example of defence policy illustrates this paradox well. Over the years, numerous reports have identified, at the minimum, defence procurement, and at the maximum all military capability, as a field where organisation at an EU level would provide the greatest savings. Yet, despite recent steps to co-ordinate some aspects of French and British policy, considerations of national sovereignty make it the field where far-reaching developments are the least likely. As the one-time British President of the European Parliament, Lord Plumb, put it in a study published in 1983, "no European defence without a federal Europe; a federal Europe is out of the question; therefore there can be no European defence".[85]

Almost as politically sensitive is the way Member States are represented in foreign capitals, and their consular services. As a result of the Lisbon Treaty, the EU now has its own European External Action Service (EEAS), with its own 'embassies' throughout the world. For the smaller EU countries at least there

---

[84] The definition of subsidiarity, and of the linked principle of proportionality, was defined in the Lisbon Treaty (Article 3b) as follows:

"Under the principle of subsidiarity, in areas which do not fall within its exclusive competence, the Union shall act only if and insofar as the objectives of the proposed action cannot be sufficiently achieved by the Member States, either at central level or at regional and local level, but can rather, by reason of the scale or effects of the proposed action, be better achieved at Union level."

"Under the principle of proportionality, the content and form of Union action shall not exceed what is necessary to achieve the objectives of the Treaties."

[85] *Thinking again about European Defence* by Hedley Bull, Col. Jonathan Alford and Dr. David Greenwood, with Foreword by Sir Henry Plumb MEP (European Democratic Group, 1983).

Understanding the EU Budget

is clearly added value in being jointly represented by the EU, rather than each having to maintain separate ambassadorial and consular services. The UK government, however, has warned that the EEAS – with the High Representative of the Union for Foreign Affairs and Security Policy, Baroness Ashton of Upholland, at its head – may indulge in 'competence creep', attempting to take over functions which should properly be the preserve of the national Foreign Office.

For Begg, in 2005 the apparent incompatibility of economic and political considerations was not quite the end of the story:

> "Even if the EU is unlikely to become even an approximation to a federal level politically, it could well be assigned more extensive public finance tasks if these could be justified on economic grounds. A lack of EU statehood or state building need not, in other words, preclude a different mix of public finances."

At the time, however, his optimism turned out to be largely misplaced: the 2007–2013 financial framework, as we have seen, changed the existing mix of public finances hardly at all. Begg was nearer the mark when remarking ruefully that "it looks increasingly likely that the EU budget will plod on along the same lines as it has since 1988...". The likelihood of the 2014–2020 Perspective doing anything very different is also slight, and certainly not as a result of a significant expansion of the Budget.

On the other hand, there are signs that some of the conclusions derived from the theories of fiscal federalism are being pursued through the alternative route of inter-governmental co-ordination, most actively within the euro area as a result of the recent debt crises. Moreover, as in the case of R&D, the Budget itself is acquiring a new role as a 'pump-primer' for investment from different sources, and as a stimulus for novel financial instruments.

Chapter 8
Conclusions

Searching finance

The subject of the European Union Budget clearly raises passions out of all proportion to its actual size. In the face of the recent proposals of the European Commission – backed for the most part by the European Parliament – for an expansion of spending which would still keep the Budget around only 1% of GDP, or 2.5% of total public expenditure, the governments of Member States have reacted with fury: how dare the EU propose increased spending, when we are all having to cut back? That the proposed added expenditure is minimal compared to what those same States were adding to their public debts not so long ago is forgotten.

Yet there are also good reasons to look at any proposed increases in the EU Budget with scepticism. The record over the years, as charted by the EU's Court of Auditors, is a shocking catalogue of waste, fraud and laxity, not fully excused by the fact that some 80% of expenditure has been administered by national, rather than EU, authorities. It is also true that the EU's institutions, like all bureaucracies, are as much interested in expanding their own powers and establishments as they are in rationally promoting public welfare. All too often it has been hard to prove that spending at EU level provides genuine added value.

Nevertheless, if one can damp down the passions and look to the future rather than the past, a good case can be made out for EU-level expenditure – not necessarily as an addition to spending at national level, but in many cases as an alternative. In purely economic terms there are savings to be made by pooling, for example, public R&D spending, and in capturing economies of scale in certain areas of public procurement. Moreover, in view of the recent manifest failure of the excessive deficit procedure introduced by the Maastricht Treaty, both the euro and the EU's general economic stability might benefit from a greater fiscal role for a central budget.

Of course, as the final section of the last chapter made clear, the EU is very far from being a United States of Europe. When it comes to national sovereignty (particularly over such sensitive issues as taxation, defence and foreign policy), politics trumps economics every time. Suppose, however, that one were starting with a clean slate, and devising a budget for a notional new 'European Union'. What changes might one make?

Expenditure

As observed by the economist Daniel Gros, quoted earlier, the CAP is in large part a legacy of Europe's post-war need to feed itself and, although now taking only 40% of the EU Budget as opposed to nearly double that not so long ago, it is the obvious first candidate for critical examination.

Until recently, the CAP supported European farming largely by supporting agricultural prices, linked to the removal of internal trade barriers. Since the reforms in the early 2000s, however, CAP spending has been increasingly tied, not to production, but to environmental considerations: for example, preservation of the countryside and of wildlife. Price support has been partly replaced by direct payments, themselves linked to ecologically responsible farming practices.

In these changed circumstances, it is reasonable to ask whether the support of agriculture – or of the rural environment – should any longer be a function carried out at EU level. Both the economics of fiscal federalism and the principle of subsidiarity indicate that it would more properly be carried out at a less centralised level: national at least, if not more local still.

A proposal to repatriate the CAP in its entirety will of course run into fierce opposition from those countries which rely heavily on EU funding, particularly, and increasingly, most of the new Member States of Central and Eastern Europe where agriculture still comprises a significant percentage of the economy (employing 18% of the workforce in Poland, for example, as compared to 2% in the UK). But here one must be rational. It is not necessary

119

to organise all agricultural support at EU level in order that Poland should have the funds to support its farmers.

The next obvious candidates for critical examination are the Structural Funds. To a significant extent, as Gros also observed, these are also a legacy of the past. The Regional and Social Funds were created at a time when the trade barriers between Member States were coming down, creating a danger of disruptions in local economies. The Single Market, however, is now much closer to completion. Moreover, as outlined earlier, the operation of the Funds has often, paradoxically, exacerbated economic distortions as Member States have promoted dubiously eligible projects in the search for *juste retour*; and there is something irrational about paying money from national budgets into the EU Budget, and then inventing schemes to get it back again. It can also be argued that, if the richer EU Member States wish to help their poorer regions or retrain the unemployed, this need not necessarily be organised at EU level either.[86]

Repatriating the bulk of the CAP, and making only demonstrably sound projects in the poorest Member States eligible for Structural Fund finance, could cut the Budget by roughly half: €60–70bn. In these times of austerity, some of this might be saved, the rest redirected towards the competitivity- and economic growth-directed policies outlined in the Lisbon Strategy and Europe 2020.

In the longer term, it might be acceptable to expand such a Budget well above the 1% of GDP ceiling which is the most Member States are currently likely to concede, and to expand its role. Budgetary participation in the creation of innovative financial instruments has been broadly welcomed by national

---

[86] It may be objected that, in default of regional policy at national level, the EU should step in to prevent a widening of regional disparities in the Union as a whole. There is certainly a case for such a 'Europe of the Regions' – but only if the EU Budget is genuinely funded by its own resources (see next section).

governments, including the UK Treasury. Even – dare one suggest it again – bonds might be issued guaranteed on the Budget, and with the interest paid out of it, to finance large-scale EU-wide projects.

Once the legacy of the past is out of the way, the future can be wide open.

The revenue side

It is difficult to disagree with the original draftsmen of the ECSC Treaty, and then of the Treaties of Rome, that the European Communities' – now the European Union's – Budget should be financed by own resources. Theoretical economics suggests that public expenditure and the taxation to fund it should be linked as closely as possible. Where institutions at one level determine expenditure, but other institutions at another level determine revenue, the first are likely to become profligate, the second niggardly.

This situation is, in practice, the one in which the EU currently finds itself. Although theoretically funded by own resources, this has always been a fraud, even when the resources included a substantial VAT element. The EU Budget is overwhelmingly funded by direct transfers from national budgets, even though the expenditure is determined at EU level by the budgetary authority: the European Parliament and the Council. Within this authority, moreover, tension has been inevitable. Whereas the Council has to look over its shoulder at the national parliaments which retain the power to tax, the European Parliament can vote to spend money knowing that the other parliaments will have to raise it.

The sensitivities of those who defend national sovereignty in the field of taxation notwithstanding, this situation should not be allowed to continue. When the EU budgetary authority votes on expenditure, it should also have to vote the necessary taxes on its own authority. The European Parliament, in particular, should acquire the historical role of all parliaments: to guard the interests of the taxpayer, and the citizen's right to the 'redress of grievances', in the face of the executive's demand for 'supply'. Were it to do so, interest in the outcome of European Elections might rise considerably.

This will mean genuine EU-level taxes. The most acceptable in the current climate of opinion would probably be those linked in some way to environmental factors: the proposed tax on internal airline flights, for example, or one directly linked to energy consumption (although the Commission has rejected these in its feasibility study). It has proposed, however, a genuine 'EU VAT' charged on non-essential items. This would provide a direct link to members of the electorate, who would observe the cost of EU spending on their VAT receipts (the administrative problems involved would be much fewer if there were a switch to the 'origin system' of charging VAT within the EU originally proposed in 1987 by the Single Market Commissioner, Lord Cockfield). A great deal of preparatory work has also been carried out by the Commission and others for the introduction of an EU-level corporation tax as an option for firms operating in several Member States. This would have a number of advantages in addition to the revenue produced (see Chapter 1), although the Commission study, rather feebly, thought it would be too difficult to get acceptance by governments and business interests.

All these possibilities, and others, are being discussed under the terms provided by Lisbon Treaty, quoted earlier. There will be considerable resistance – as there is to all proposals for new taxes. Much will turn on the detailed calculations which each national treasury will make: is the revenue raised in each country likely to be more or less than the savings made from no longer having to make transfers to the EU out of the national budgets? Several past proposals for EU taxes – for example, that for a tax on CO_2 emissions – came to nothing as a result of opposition from national governments or special interests. This is no reason, however, why a serious effort now should not succeed.

These 'clean slate' proposals, individually, will not find much favour with any established schools of thought on EU matters. Eurosceptics will support repatriation of the CAP and the Structural Funds, but not EU-level taxes. Federalists may like the taxes, but probably not an end to half traditional EU spending.

As a linked package of measures, however, there might just be a chance of acceptance. It is worth trying.

Bibliography

Balfe, Richard: in *Memories of the first elected European Parliament* (Allendale, 2007).

Begg, Prof. Iain: *Funding the European Union* (Federal Trust, March 2005).

Commission: *Stable Money – Sound Finances: Community public finance in the perspective of EMU* (*European Economy*, no. 53, 1993).

Commission: *Commission Regulation (EC, EURATOM) No 2342/ 2002 of 23 December 2002 laying down detailed rules for the implementation of Council Regulation (EC, Euratom) No 1605/2002 on the Financial Regulation applicable to the general budget of the European Communities* (OJL 357, 31.12.2002,OJL 248, 16.9.2002, p. 1.)

Commission: *Proposal for a Council Decision on the system of the European Communities' own resources* (COM(2004)501 of 3.8.2004).

Commission: *The EU Budget Review: Communication from the Commission to the European Parliament, the Council, the European Economic and Social Committee, the Committee of the Regions and national parliaments* (COM(2010)700 final).

Commission: *Europe 2020: A European strategy for smart, sustainable and inclusive growth* (COM(2010)2020 of 3.3.2010).

Commission: *Proposal for a Regulation of the European Parliament and of the Council on the Financial Regulation applicable to the general budget of the European Union* (COM(2010) 260 final of 28 May 2010).

Commission: *Quantifying the potential macroeconomic effects of the Europe 2020 strategy: stylised scenarios* (European Commission Economic Papers n°424. September 2010) and *Macroeconomic effects of Europe 2020: stylised scenarios* (ECFIN Economic Briefs 2010 n°11).

Commission: *A Budget for Europe 2020: Communication from the Commission to the European Parliament, the Council, the European Economic and Social Committee and the Committee of the Regions* (COM(2011) 500 final, 29.6.2011).

Commission: *Financing the EU Budget: report on the operation of the own resources system* (Commission Staff Working Paper SEC(2011) 876 final of 29.6.2 011).

Committee of Independent Experts: *First Report on Allegations regarding Fraud, Mismanagement and Nepotism in the European Commission* (Office for Official Publications of the European Communities, 15 March 1999).

Committee of Independent Experts: *Second Report on Reform of the Commission: Analysis of current practice and proposals for tackling mismanagement, irregularities and fraud* (Office for Official Publications of the European Communities, 10 September 1999).

Council of Ministers: *Conclusions of the Council on the measures necessary to guarantee the effective implementation of the conclusions of the European Council on Budgetary Discipline* (10446/84).

Council of Ministers: *Council Regulation (EC, Euratom) No 1605/2002 on the Financial Regulation applicable to the general budget of the European Communities* (OJL 357, 31.12.2002,OJL 248, 16.9.2002, p. 1.)

Court of Auditors: *Reports* (1977, 1978, 1979, 1980, 1986, 1987, 1990, 1991, 1992, 1993, 1994, 1995, 1997, 1998, 1999, 2000, 2001, 2006, 2009).

Court of Auditors: *Opinion on a proposal for a regulation of the European Parliament and of the Council on the Financial Regulation applicable to the general budget of the European Union* (Opinion No 6/2010).

Court of Justice (ECJ): *Application for annulment relating to the legality of the general budget of the European Communities for the financial year 1986* (Judgment of 3.7.1986 — CASE 34/86).

Elles MEP, James (*rapporteur*): *Report on the accounts of the European Communities in respect of the 1996 financial year* (20 April 1999 A4-0196/99, PE 230.655 final).

European Council: *Presidency conclusions following the Fontainebleau European Council* (1984).

European Council: *Presidency Conclusions to the Lisbon European Council, 23 and 24 March 2000.*

European Parliament: *Flexibility in the Multiannual Financial Framework 2007 – 2013: revisions and use of instruments* (Directorate-General for Internal Policies, October 2010).

Financial Times: 'EU growth funds lie idle under red tape' (29 November 2010).

Garriga Polledo MEP, Salvador (*rapporteur*): *Investing in the future: a new Multiannual Financial Framework (MFF) for a competitive, sustainable and inclusive Europe* (European Parliament, 27 May 2011, PE458.649. A7-0193/2011).

Gros, Daniel: *How to Achieve a Better Budget for the European Union* (Centre for European Policy Studies, 2008).

House of Commons: *Fifth Report from the Treasury and Civil Service Committee of the House of Commons: Budgetary Discipline in the European Community* (HMSO, 21 April 1986).

House of Lords Select Committee on the European Union: *Inquiry on EU Financial Framework from 2014: Evidence Session No.2.* (18 January 2011).

MacDougall, Sir Donald (chairman): *Report of the Study Group on the Role of Public Finance in European Integration, Vol.1: General Report* (Office for Official Publications of the European Communities, April 1977).

Patterson, Ben: *Purse-strings of Europe*: *the European Parliament and the Community Budget* (London Office of the European Parliament, 1979).

Plumb, Sir Henry MEP: Foreword to *Thinking again about European Defence* by Hedley Bull, Col. Jonathan Alford and Dr. David Greenwood (European Democratic Group, 1983).

Ruding, Onno: *Conclusions and Recommendations of the Committee of Independent Experts on Company Taxation* (Commission, 1992).

Servan-Schreiber, Jean-Jacques: *Le Défi Americain* (Denoël, 1967).

Shaw, Michael MP: *The European Parliament and the Community Budget* (European Conservative Group, June 1978).

Tanzi, Vito: *On fiscal federalism: issues to worry about* (IMF, 2000).

UK Government: *The United Kingdom and the European Communities* (Cmnd. 4715, HMSO July 1971).